W9-ACW-861

PEACE IS OUR PROFESSION

OUR statements often say
what governments should
do, or chiefs of state or
heads of churches. But few
of us state what we are
willing to do.   M. Buber

"Peace Is Our Profession" was adopted by the Strategic Air Command of the U.S. Air Force as a Cold War slogan for its nuclear bomb-laden squadrons poised to incinerate half the earth as part of the Pentagon's MAD [Mutual Assured Destruction] strategy for a *"balance of terror"* with its military mirror image in the Soviet Union. Refitted with conventional high explosive ordinance, SAC B-52 bombers were diverted to carpet bomb missions over Vietnam, Cambodia and Laos at the height of the Indochina War, spearheading a decade-long bombing campaign more explosive than any previous bombardment in history.

PEACE IS OUR PROFESSION

Poems and Passages

of War Protest

Edited by Jan Barry

East River Anthology

Library of Congress Catalog No.: 80-70115
ISBN: 0-917238-03-6

Printed in the United States of America
Calligraphy on front flyleaf by Daniel Berrigan
Cover photo by Paul Tick
Typesetting by WIN Magazine
Printed by Faculty Press

Every effort has been made to trace ownership of all copyrighted material and to secure permission to publish. In the event of any oversight or other error, the editor extends deep apologies and will gladly make any necessary corrections in future printings.

Grateful thanks are extended to all the contributors to this volume, and to the many more unsung supporters of this project, with formal acknowledgement to the following authors and publishers:

Denise Levertov: "In Thai Binh (Peace) Province" from *The Freeing of the Dust*, © 1975 by New Directions. "The Day the Audience Walked Out on Me, and Why" from *Footprints*, © 1972 by Denise Levertov. Selections from *To Stay Alive*, © 1970 by Denise Levertov. Reprinted by permission of New Directions.

Hayden Carruth: "The Birds of Vietnam" from *From Snow and Rock, From Chaos*, © 1973 by Hayden Carruth. Reprinted by permission of New Directions Publishing Corp.

William G. Kelsey: "To Learn from Hiroshima," Reprinted by permission from *The Progressive*, © 1977 by The Progressive Inc.

Peter Berenbak: "With Peace Comes Reality." Reprinted by permission from the Sunday, May 11, 1975 *Daily Record* of Morristown, N.J.

Wendell Berry: "Dark with Power" from *Openings*, © 1968 by Wendell Berry. Reprinted by permission of Harcourt Brace Jovanovich, Inc.

Richard Boyle: Selections from *Flower of the Dragon*, © 1972 by Ramparts Press. Reprinted by permission of Ramparts Press, Palo Alto, CA. 94303

Milton Mayer: Selections reprinted by permission from *The Progressive*, © 1980 by The Progressive, 408 W. Gorham St., Madison, WI 53703.

Additional acknowledgements are contained in the "Biographical Notes" section at the back of the book.

I cannot keep silent:
For I hear the sound of the trumpet,
The alarm of war.

Disaster upon disaster,
The whole land laid waste...
How long must I see the war standard,
Hear the sound of the trumpet?

Jeremiah 4:19-21

FOR THE CHILDREN OF THE WORLD

War   When
bugles   will
call   it
from   end,
every   this
city   loud
wall.   tragic
*   music?*

Tu Fu

INTRODUCTION

Reviving the eloquence and outrage from the peace marches, sit-ins, teach-ins, speak-outs and often lonely vigils of the Vietnam War era, this anthology is intended to be a sort of reader of revolt to hand the next generation being wooed into witless war.

The focus of this collective challenge to the power of war is two-fold: one aim is to illuminate the force of language, the often overlooked sparks of words that ignite explosions of human action, inflame passions for war or peace. The other aim is frankly to startle or enchant or draw the reader stone sober into listening to how humans struggle for survival, yet often fail to communicate, shouting past each others' speech, blundering into war, blundering out again, blaming others but seldom reexamining our own responsibility.

Here are poems and prose passages, selections from letters, diaries and speeches, photographs and artwork by Americans and Vietnamese, soldiers and civilians, men and women, which do reach out to others, trying to bridge the irresponsible abyss of war.

Listening to the words we use is often the first clue to what we indeed do. That is perhaps the secret gift poets and social gadflies are blessed with, and try to share with societies which often seem deaf to the stark horrors of commonplace speech, especially in wartime. Despite the official explanation that American soldiers went to Southeast Asia to aid a clutch of beleaguered allies, when I arrived in Vietnam as a soldier in December 1962 the term most frequently heard among oldtimers in the American expeditionary force regarding Asians was "gooks" — a contemptuous salute which had been slung around for generations by cynical overseas GIs.

Vietnamese in particular were also referred to as "slopes" and "slopeheads," and later "dinks," which rhymed with "chinks," GI slang in the Korean War.

So much for the official line that Americans loved these Asian peoples betrayed by our soldiers' slang. To learn why we were engaged in yet another Asian battlezone, the rawest recruit in Indochina needed only to listen to our barracks language (with its hoary echoes from previous wars): "The only good gook (good Indian). . . is a dead gook (dead Indian)." A good trooper was always "gung-ho," a Chinese aphorism picked up by the American expeditionary force in China back at the turn of the century. Older Vietnamese men and women, often pressed into service as barracks servants, were addressed as "papa-san" and "mama-san," GI pidgin phrases from occupation duty in Japan after World War II. As could be expected, many Vietnamese returned our fantastic contempt, treating us like previous (French, Japanese, Chinese) invaders.

Yet other Vietnamese and something indescribable in Vietnam (where I spent 10 months as a soldier) turned my life around, propelling me to resign the next year from the corps of cadets at West Point, throw up an intended military career, and seek to master the mysteries of writing in order to recount that unsettling experience — and, further, to seek out the peace movement to add my protest of the mushrooming war and learn what I could from peacemakers.

Along the way, I met many others reaching out of the war, determined to be both survivors and recorders of that experience but also trailblazers toward a better way. As was true of the two previous anthologies I was involved in (*Winning Hearts & Minds: War Poems by Vietnam Veterans* and *Demilitarized Zones: Veterans After Vietnam*], this collection is very much a creation of its literary contributors, with the aid of many generous friends.

The international peace movement this book represents was a beacon light not only in the midst of the Indochina War nightmare but in the war carnage history of "civilization." Yet this protest movement has received scant attention in American cultural re-creations of that war. Numerous books, films and plays have presented various versions of the horror of the Indochina warfare, but few have focused on the work of those who struggled to end the holocaust.

This circumstance has not come about by accident.

"After every war in which Americans have fought, history textbooks have interpreted that war to succeeding generations," write William L. Griffen and John Marciano, in a detailed expose of U.S. high school history textbooks titled *Teaching the Vietnam War.* "Interpretations in the past have always stressed the necessity of our involvement and defended the correctness and morality of America's wartime role," they note.

Not only textbook publishers, but American media of every sort and Ronald Reagan's recent presidential campaign have worked hard to bury our atrocities in Southeast Asia, presenting our massacres there as a "noble" failure.

Against that blind mindlessness pushing to whitewash and rewrite history, this anthology also presents work illuminating the on-going revolt against war makers since the Indochina holocaust, as well as that of prophetic voices who long ago challenged the broken record bugle call for military crusades in the immediate aftermath of WWII: when Indochina's long agony began (as U.S. "Liberty" ships returned French colonial troops to Vietnam) in the shadow of the mushroom cloud drifting off Hiroshima — a cloud threatening still to end us all.

Montclair, N.J.
November 1980

Jan Barry

FOREWORD

The Vietnamese love poetry. Their culture is best understood by their poems. Though Vietnamese recognize the superior talent of their especially gifted poets and songwriters, they do not consider poetry and song to be the special property of a small group of literati. They are for everyone. Farmers, soldiers, and students all write poems.

The interest in poetry is part of the Vietnamese love of beauty, their devotion to aesthetics, which is evident in their approach to the spiritual as well as the physical world. They are fond of saying of a particularly courageous and inspiring person that his life was like a poem. Nowhere are poetry and life more closely intertwined than in Viet Nam.

But few outsiders have read the poems and understood the culture of Viet Nam. Few have listened to the voices of the people of Viet Nam.

We may tire when we hear continually of poor suffering Viet Nam, but one must remember that Vietnamese could not avoid the war. In the poem "The Present," a poet tells of sitting down to write his girlfriend a love letter but finds the words "I love" slanted by the explosions of rockets, shaking his hand holding the pen. He ends by saying "Some day when there's peace/I will write you a different poem."

When one considers all that has happened to Viet Nam, it is remarkable that Vietnamese have not lost their ability to hope. In a collection of songs called "Songs from the Devastated Fields," Mien Duc Thang, a popular young songwriter and singer, expressed what had happened to his land and people. Mien Duc Thang was put in prison by the Thieu regime for singing these songs, but he did not give in to despair.

> From the devastated fields of today
>   We sing these songs;
> Despite a thousand frightful years
>   our life is still happy,
> Though weariness is printed on our dry hands,
> We will never give up. . .

So let us go and recultivate our fields,
So we can live and die in our homeland;
And tomorrow our land will flourish
      with new ricefields,
Tomorrow our land will blossom with
      more smiles,
Tomorrow our land will be greener than
      the mountains and hills,
For tomorrow we are determined to live
      in our land.

In the West we are taught to suspect those who wear their hearts on their sleeves. Many of us cling to the belief that an emotional cry from the heart should be restrained and are ashamed or reluctant to give in to our true feelings. With us there is the real danger that the levels of self-control we achieve may make us forget the validity of the feeling they are designed to mask. And it is wrong, it would seem, for Americans who can absorb the horrors of a My Lai and saturation bombing of a land and people with only ripples of   guilt in the national consciousness to pass judgement on people who have not lost their capacity to weep in the face of suffering. These poems are affirmations of feelings on the part of a people who have long been treated by many Americans as if they had no feelings. By reading their poetry we can learn what has happened to them, and hopefully, what has happened to us.

Don Luce
John C. Schafer
Jacquelyn Chagnon

Adapted from the introduction to We Promise One Another: Poems of an Asian War *(Indochina Mobile Education Project, 1971)*

I work in a library and the other day a young boy came up to the counter, his hands full of big books of battles and guns. Expecting, I'm sure, a smile from me. . . he said, his eyes glowing, ''I love war!''

For a moment I almost returned what he expected, out of the polite habit one develops working in such a place. But instead I looked at him and said, ''I'm sorry to hear that.'' His face fell.

But wouldn't it have been meaningful to hand him (this) anthology. . .

Rachelle Benveniste
Culver City, California

MAGIC FLOWERS

These are presents
from our friends in outer space.
They say, ''Dear people on Earth.
You have too many wars.
These will stop the wars.
These are magic flowers.''

Kim Crumb
Age 6

PEACE IS OUR PROFESSION

Why is it that the beauty of the world
excites in some people a rage to rape to ruin,
a terrible desire to trample and uproot
the garden from which humanity grew...

Conquistador, would you tear the hair from your
grandmother's head?
Soldier, would you assault your mother?

Defoliated tree, South China Sea, Vietnam.

"In spring 1969 the 101st (Airborne Division) began its most ambitious attempts to pacify northern I Corps by moving into the communists' mountain base camps and supply areas. Here, in the mysterious tangled jungles of the mountains and valleys just east of Laos, was the key to the security of the entire region. And here the 101st first subdued and then tamed the famous A Shau Valley. . . The valley that had been a sanctuary for the communist forces since the days of French rule was dramatically transfigured as helicopters roamed the valley and Screaming Eagles pushed through the lush vegetation, seeking out the enemy. . .

"The invasion and conquest of the A Shau have become a part of division legend to live on alongside the great campaigns of World War II. . . (In September 1969, the last battalion pulled out,) completing the withdrawal of division troops from the valley.

"Infantry and artillery raids into the valley would continue, blocking any communist attempts to reassert their control of the strange and beautiful landscape that Screaming Eagles had subdued."

1968-69 Pictorial Review of the 101st Airborne Division in Vietnam

violence
dog tags
red dirt
shit
olive drab
baggy pants
with baggy pockets
gook
napalm
SP/4
Ban Me Thout
Boun Ho, Ban Don
garbage
gonorrhea
grenades
siren
death
    quick death
    slow death
    crippling death
    permanent death
    $10,000
Air America, CIA
easy money
black market
number one
beaucoup fear
beaucoup anger

bullet
pain
chopper
miniguns
mistakes

1900 hours
operation
search and destroy
contact
CIB
Lifer
career soldier
Man In Service To His Country
Yours is but to do or die
    die
55,000 American lives
Fifty-Five Thousand men
died in this country
for a rotten jungle
full of
    booby traps
    snipers
    mines
    rockets
    and other absurdities

James D. Lange

Orange Truth

101st Airborne Division walks through defoliated area of Vietnam in 1969 during Operation Apache Snow.

Ridgeline on rim of A Shau Valley (U.S. Army photograph)

rsation, but it

d begun inves-
des on behalf
eran who died
blamed on
in Vietnam,''
unt.

my handwrit-
veteran's per-
it up and cir-
s. "It's almost
Al Young gave
emo appeared
rsion, possibly
dquarters, she

e prepared, at
superiors, two
on the health
er of Vietnam
ht might have
rbicide poison-
sponse — and
s harrassment
ears'' after she
bout Agent Or-
television sta-

at initial news
CBS-affiliate
1978, VA head-
a frenzy of ac-
ide controver-

ctor's original
from October
a member of
yet another

ited version is
presented only

n advised that
Hand'' veter-
d a "high con-
of the defoli-
ted that a $300
was currently
court in Arizo-
e family of a
d of cancer af-
to herbicides
. Forest Serv-

bserving these
extreme con-
orable decision

health concerns, the first of several Vietnam veterans filed a law-
suit against Do
a suit which h
billion class ac
a number of ch
herbicide manufacturers, in turn,
have filed a countersuit against
the government, claiming that
they provided Agent Orange as
specified in government contracts
and have no responsibility for how
it was used in Vietnam.

Concern over the possible mag-
nitude of Agent Orange claims
was written by the VA benefits
section into the file of the Vietnam
veteran whose widow first raised
the herbicide-poisoning question,

service-related, she recalls. But a
note was put in the man's file
re was no way to
claims, that it
mically unfeasi-
ctor.

VA headquarters refused to provide the **Daily Record** with copies
of DeVictor's 1977 reports on
Agent Orange or to explain how
the agency responded to these reports.

"The bottom line is dollars,"
says Dr. Bogen, the former VA
hospital chief of staff. "The average length of time per (compensa-
tion) claim is 113 years, with de-
pendents, children. It's a nightmare of money."

A thousand years of Chinese reign,
A hundred years of French domain,
Twenty years of American intervention
The heritage of our Motherland,
A forest of dry bones,
The heritage of our Motherland,
A mountain of graves...

Teach children the sound of truth,
For the mother hopes her children won't forget their race,
Their ancestors who built the old Viet Nam;
She waits for her children to come home,
She waits for all her children who are far away,
For all her children who have the same father,
Wherever they are
They must forget how to hate.

A thousand years of Chinese reign,
A hundred years of French domain,
Twenty years of American intervention
The heritage of our Motherland,
Dry and barren ricefields,
The heritage of our Motherland,
Rows of burned houses...

Trinh Cong Son

Life is precarious enough,
a leaf on the sea
before a storm.
Yet some men shorten it still,
stirring up wars.

Sleep well, sleep well, my son.
Tomorrow you become a young man.
You'll carry sword and gun.

Sleep well, sleep well, my son.
When you become a young man,
You'll kill your friends and brothers.

Sleep well, sleep well, my son.
Tomorrow when you become a young man,
You'll not sleep well again.

Do Nghe

"Vietnamese belong in school, not in the army"
says a vietnamese lad who is at least not
a fool
            Apathy: antithesis of hope, axiom of war
            M16s
            M2s
            M1s
            Grenade launchers
                This baby will knock a man
                off his feet at 300 yards

APCs
tanks
AKs
B4Os
dope
Tet
7 days, no sleep
marginal victory
Freedom for the People
        who?
The people that died

James D. Lange

They are called *My*
Which my brother says means beautiful.
But they are not beautiful:
They have too much hair on their arms like monkeys,
They are tall like trees without branches,
Their eyes are green like eyes of boiled pigs
In the markets during the New Year.
Their hair is blonde and not black
Their skin is pink and not brown,
Their cars frighten cyclists in the streets,
Their "flying machines" and their "dragonflies"
Drop death on people and animals
And make trees bare of their leaves.
Here, Americans are not beautiful.
"But they are,
In their far away country,"
My brother says.

Hoang Son
Age 14

Saigon

My (Me-e): Vietnamese term for Americans

Hot morning,
the drift of temple bells,
of schoolgirls' chatter
in a gentle language GIs don't use or listen to:
it's too quiet, too peaceful
beyond this boring bunker and its gun happy crew
which eyes the children, thirsty for targets. . .
as teenage gate guards snicker
("Hey you baby-san, hey you boom-boom?")
     daring lusty conquests of these still
     budding lotus flower females,
     as jumpy GIs daydream drunk on war.

We shoot the sick, the young, the lame,
We do our best to kill and maim,
Because the kills count all the same,
Napalm sticks to kids.

Ox cart rolling down the road,
Peasants with a heavy load,
They're all VC when the bombs explode,
Napalm sticks to kids.

A baby sucking on his mother's tit,
Children cowering in a pit,
Dow Chemical doesn't give a shit,
Napalm sticks to kids.

Blues out on a road recon,
See some children with their mom,
What the hell, let's drop the bomb,
Napalm sticks to kids.

Flying low across the trees,
Pilots doing what they please,
Dropping frags on refugees,
Napalm sticks to kids.

CIA with guns for hire,
Montagnards around a fire,
Napalm makes the fire higher,
Napalm sticks to kids…

Composed by GIs of the 1st Air Cavalry Div. in Vietnam

VC: Viet Cong, Vietnamese Communists

The village school of Ky Phu, south Vietnam, after ''pacification'' of the village by Phantom jet fighter-bombers out of the U.S. Marine base at Chu Lai [July 1967].

On this land
      Where each blade of grass is human hair
Each foot of soil is human flesh
      Where it rains blood
Hails bones
      Life must flower

Ngo Vinh Long

Comfortable people do not look.
Murder is not nice business.
Let soldiers do your work.
All that horror is for peace.

Put a label on the victims of our crimes.
Call them commies, dinks or dupes.
They're not human anymore.
They must be die or be degraded.

They have no dreams.
They feel no pain.
They're just gooks and slopes,
Objects for our jokes.

Joseph M. Shea

Listen to this:
yesterday six Vietcong came through my village.
Because of this my village was bombed--completely destroyed.
Every soul was killed. . .

Whoever is listening, be my witness!
I cannot accept this war.
I never could, I never shall.
I must say this a thousand times before I am killed.

I feel I am like that bird which dies for the sake of its mate,
dripping blood from its broken beak and crying out:
Beware! Turn around to face your real enemies--
ambition, violence, hatred, greed.

Men cannot be our enemies--even men called 'Vietcong!'
If we kill men, what brothers will we have left?
With whom shall we live then?

Thich Nhat Hanh

February 12. This battle probably hit the news. Enough people died to satisfy the press. It's a sickening thought as I watch the helicopters carry the bodies. . . But I admire the spirit of the V.C. But who wouldn't have spirit? They have a cause to die for, it's their country. We have nothing to gain. We don't even want the country. So what is to win--when we have nothing to win?

Feb. 19.

The sonless father.
A pile of stones,
a lonely heart,
on blood soiled ground,
I play the part
of the fool patriot
     without a cause.
A clear conscience,
a closed mind,
this ignorant patriot
sees, but is blind
to what really is,
     and now was.
I hate not these people,
I hate not the land,
I hate but the person
with his peace waving hand
starts a war and wants
everyone else to fight it.

 Mar. 20. Looking back through the pages, I can now make a statement on all the facts I have thus far collected. . . That is, I've been here 6 months and still don't know what the hell we're fighting for.

April 1. I no longer care why it's happening. I just want to stop it, or it to stop. . . Fighting in the name of peace. Every time I say that it gets more ridiculous.

April 8. The early hour of the morn. A stillness, peace and tranquility. The funky wild birds echo their caws across the valley. A slight mist covers the ground. . .A new day, new trials. It feels so beautiful. . . Just for these few hours I feel the freedom of thought, and the closeness of nature. But also I feel the loss of having no one to share it with. The early hours of the morn, these few hours, it's all I've got--the rest of the day belongs to the war lords.

Bruce Anello
Killed in Vietnam
31 May 1968

Shell gasoline station in Tam Ky, south Vietnam

They will not forget us,
not a hundred thousand generations
after our dark angel
swoops down like a pterodactyl.
Such cunning, they'll think,
& such a taste for blood.
Who would have believed it
of a little biped.

They will not forget us.
They will drag us out of our graves,
out of our wretched mudholes,
scrape our bones from the earth,
preserve us--
place us beside our arrowheads
& pots.

Steve Kowit

If war is hell
(as General Sherman spat)
then we who were soldiers
created it.

Photos in preceding series by Doug Hostetter,
Poems in italics by Jan Barry.

August 6, 1945

Fred Braun has just leaned out on a low windowsill
that needs painting. There are cracks in it,
but so far they have let no rain through.
They can wait a little longer.
This moment is his to enjoy,
looking at his apple orchard and two small plum trees
and under them a red napkin of bee balm.
It is beautiful and peaceful. His wife
is troweling a flower bed
along the house wall. He hears
the thud of an apple falling, marking
the nice lethargy of the day.
And exactly now, across the world,
behind a plane, the *Enola Gay*,
there falls a thin tube
with a small fuse at one end
that will fire one of two parts
into the larger part at the other end
and explode this filament
with a light brighter than the sun. Below,
in the wooden city Hiroshimá
can it not be that a man
has just rolled back
one of his living-room shutters
and is looking out on his garden, thinking,
The morning glories on their bamboo sticks,
the blue sky,
how beautiful everything is! Let me enjoy it.
I should be painting the shutters,
but they can wait.
The rain does not yet come through.

Millen Brand

from ENOLA GAY

Can we speak of the flesh falling from bones
the roaring of matter torn
as loud as the horror screams
deep into the ears
of a hundred thousand burning souls?
The flash, the river, the blast, the storm,
and the sickness
the long slow radiating pain
that will stalk a thousand hallways
into now
and lie in the cribs of the future.
The horror of 8:15
will tear at a billion dreams
and from the ash two figures wake:
the frail bird of peace
and the beast of wild abandon
and to the agony chorus they sing:
fly away enola gay
you've done enough today.

Return to base.
Circle back to the nest
and the wicked wind
that blows
upon the upper deck.
There waits your fearful eggs
that will mutate on into decades.
The props and clocks turn round and . ɐ d
as you pass the battles of boundry
the fight for the flesh and blood
of the Earth
from which you sprang.
The weapons you hold
are the essence of matter itself
the children who would turn upon their mother
the mad fetus
that would tear the very womb
that holds it.
Let your eggs go cold and useless
fall into the sea and just decay
fly no more
enola gay.

Don Ogden

ON A BRIDGE AT HIROSHIMA

a flat black shadow
etched into the solid
stone   had arms outflung
and feet running forward,
as welcome to our future.

R.B. Weber

DARK GROWTH

We were trained to watch for
Epimetheus' jar or Pandora's box
and sat smuggly alert
with our silhouette books

for slant-eyed, fire-haired demons
we could fight on common ground,

but one clear summer morning
made for butterflies, kites,
and lovers on hills,

jar and box were spilled
from the belly of the Enola Gay;
now mushrooms grow in darkness
and summer dims to memory
under winter skies.

Margaret Key Biggs

(U.S. Air Force photograph)

THE WAKE OF THE SECOND WORLD WAR

"When I saw those bloated generals riding down Broadway, gloating in their triumph, and a million screaming fools fawning at their feet because they had been successful in killing a considerable portion of the world's population, I knew mankind hadn't changed an iota from the days of the Roman conqueror, who strutted in triumph through the streets with his slaves at his chariot wheels. That is what people love, one man's glory and a million dead!

"I was in the army for three years and never met a dozen who were willing to be there. . . It made no difference that we thought we had inalienable rights. All the Declarations of Independence and Rights of Man ever written are so much paper to regimenters. Laws are dumb in the midst of arms. Then when it is all over, and the generals and politicians who manuevered the whole thing get together, they try to smooth things out. They stand up before the million men who came home broken and embittered, and the ghosts of as many who died, and you hear words like we heard this afternoon:

" 'They gave their all,' says the one who made the law that gave them their choice between Leavenworth and the army. 'They gave their lives,' says the one who drove them into battle and death. 'They gave the last full measure of devotion,' says the one who inaugurated this system in America. They gave nothing! They went with a gun in their backs. And now they are going to start it all over again. The same ruthless tyranny. . . Enslavement for the purpose of murder!

"The radio, the press and motion pictures are already in it up to their necks, preaching hate and prejudice. Watch the priest take it to the pulpit, and the politician to the senate. All working to prepare the public mind for that state where war becomes inevitable. Put them in the stage of hysteria where anyone who dares oppose their violence will be fuel for the fires of persecution. God, the incredible flood of propoganda that deluges the earth every day, designed to make one half the world hate the other half! Is there any greater crime against humanity?"

Robert Baker Elder

from WHOM THE GODS DESTROY [A novel]

WHAT THE ARMY BUILDS

The slogan at the recruiting station is "The Army Builds Men." The slogan is a scream. It's as if the state penitentiary advertised free steak dinners without specifying that in order to be eligible you had to be scheduled to be hanged the next morning. What the Army builds is one-legged men, and dead men.

The slogan is even more crooked than that. The condemned convict actually gets the steak dinner, but the soldier, who is ultimately going to get his head full of holes, does not even get built into a man in the intervening period.

One way in which the Army builds men is to put them into an environment where the venereal disease rate is 29.6 cases per 1,000 compared with 5.1 among civilians. (The Navy builds even handsomer men, with a venereal disease rate of 85.8.) Peacetime admission of civilians to mental hospitals is 299.1 per 100,000; of soldiers, 950. Peacetime civilian suicides are 14.2 per 100,000; peacetime soldier suicides, 29.

The Army builds dead men and has never built anything else—any army, anywhere, ever. The proper business of the Army is not physical training, or education, or travel, or companionship, or the life of Reilly. The proper business of the Army is killing, and the only thing it can properly build is killers and killees.

Since the Army does not build men, nobody who wants to be a man should ever join the Army. Anybody who wants to be a man should keep out of the Army, whatever else he may do. Since a man does not run away, he should not run away from the Army. He should fight it.

Milton Mayer

in The Progressive
September 22, 1947

POST SCRIPT

In 1918—we had just licked the Prussians—Woodrow Wilson called peacetime conscription "the root evil of Prussianism." In 1945 we licked the Prussians again, and in 1948 I'm a son-of-a-gun if we didn't get peacetime conscription. Each time we lick the Prussians we get to be more like them. Maybe we won't lick them the next time around. . . and get to be less like them.

Milton Mayer

in The Progressive
June 1980

ANCIENT FRAGMENT FROM THE EDGE OF THE EMPIRE

Korea, 1952

At ease, gentlemen. Let's keep it brief. This map
gives our share of the ridge: markings in blue,
our howitzers and 8-inch pieces. Lacking radios
the enemy's greater numbers are noise, launching ranks
straight ahead on bugle signals, hand-sirens,
even bells. We own the air. That forces them
into attacks by night, with only their first 2 waves
coming armed. Their 3rd and 4th bear scythes, hooks,
farm tools, sticks. Their 5th waves carry nothing.
Remind your men 8th Army is fully behind us.
Later today, my G4 will have details on the R&R
we're awarding 6 kills confirmed.

Despite problems last night, mainly we held.
The altered map updates positions. Notice where
Division Rear is doubling artillery support.
During the breakthrough Tyler kept his head
like a soldier, calling in fire on his own bunkers.
We killed 10 to 1 but their later waves picked up
rifles and handguns, advancing. Temporarily
Battalion Medical will re-group back to Wonju.
Stop your men shooting rats by explaining
how the fever spreads through vermin deserting
the carcases. With perimeters fluid, be sure
all squads get late changes in password. Tyler
knew none of our officers has ever been captured
and I'm putting him in for a Silver Star. Now G4,
with one or two changes on ammo and food.

Word on the fever seems good: 8th Army's near
to a cure. Warn units that self-inflicted wounds
equal refusal to serve; and post reliable guards
on water
cooled 30-calibres which, as we know,
will heat and jam when drunk dry. Our magnesium flares
last night lit up hordes of their dead littering
assault routes, though by this morning
the bodies were gone. With so much ammo showing
corrosion, check boxes for date. Take names
of men pocketing leaflets that offer soft terms
for surrender, and remind each man 1st Battalion
has never abandoned its wounded. Later, possibly
today, G4 will explain the new situation on water.

Reg Saner

from AMERICAN VOICES

Winter left us
    with thundering casualty lists in our ears
        from Iwo Jima and Hiroshima —
    and a new love of peace.
May dug us a grave in Laurel, Mississippi..
    His last letter:
        ''They are going to take my life
        to keep the Negro down in
        the South. Keep on fighting.''
           Willie McGee

Spring investigated our street,
    found pavement breaking into daylight,
        the Tree of Heaven in our alley
           yawning and stretching
and one of us poking for treasure in our trash heaps.

The morning is beautiful, Spring said,
    If dogs don't bark at you
        and police don't hanker after you
and you sleep the lingering hours into sunlight,
    your bed supported by sixteen million Americans.

        ''. . . America's approach to the colonial
           races is to treat them as if they were
           not human. . . Now we are reaping what
           we have sown. Many in America feel
           they are better than Asians; better
           than the darker races; better than the
           Jews.'' — *Signed:* Mrs. I.W. Epps
                The News Leader, Richmond, Va.

Spring swore out a warrant for breach of peace,
    declaring:
        This sleeping street is what one sees and smells,
        plus a jellied gasoline bomb the street knows
        only from a newspaper dispatch:

            "Inhabitants asphyxiated in the exact posture
            they held when struck, one woman reading her
            Sears-Roebuck catalog, in a little hamlet north
            on Anyang, the torn page crayoned on mail
            order No. 3,811,294: 'a bewitching bedjacket,
            coral.' "

Your morning was like this, neighbor,
    your naked sleep clothed with the most precious
        grammar to spell out how your flesh shines
        like a song that sings in your own words:

            Courier Journal, Louisville, Kentucky:
            "I saw two brothers come home. . . for the
            older, war is forever over. As the flag-
            draped coffin was taken from the train,
            what could the younger boy, who
            had escorted his brother 8,000 miles, say to
            his parents? What could the President say
            if he had been standing there?. . .
                              H.D.L.

Between your own letters to the editor, neighbor,
    Spring spoke its own plain song:
        Soldier, brother, son,
            Whose Bunker Hill is this mountain top
        you clutched so quietly?
        Who owns this blade of grass
        you stained with your dying sweat?
        How do you spell the name of the village
        whose housetops you lifted with your trigger?

            The Post, Denver, Colorado:
            "Here is the story of a lonely soldier. . .
            with a dream of brother love and peace
            some day not so far away
            from this world of today. . .
            P.S. Pray for us out here. . . We need it."
                        PFC Ed Gallegos

What recording sings as these letters do
    just as they were written,
        an epic of the long journey you made
from Indianapolis and Frisco

to land on someone else's island
and kill many strangers,
until you were overpowered by their love of land and
died clutching this strange hill?
Whose sweetheart will plant flowers in your helmet?
Whose mothers will rock their babies to sleep
with lullabies of your coming and going?
Which man's father hails you as liberator?
Who will tell the young warriors
sleeping on the hillsides of Gettysburg
that you loved their hollowed cries?

    Seattle Times, Seattle, Washington:
    ''. . . all men are our brothers; a common
    doom confronts us all.''
                  Dorothy K. Schmidt

Brother, soldier, son:
All around you are voices of Spring
everyone can hear singing.

    Evening Bulletin, Philadelphia, Pennsylvannia:
    ''I am 12 years old. There is something
    puzzling me and I thought maybe you could
    help me. If you can, please tell me why
    people want to construct such destructive
    things as bombs.''
              Caryn Colinati

Now the milkman drives his chariot down our street,
his trumpeting bottles alert our doorsteps
for another day.
The sun pours out on the neighbor's cyclamen bush
a million degrees of exploding atomic heat
and filters through 2,000 million human volts
one more morning of pursuit of liberty and peace. . .
Across the coral isthmus Korea,
across the human isthmus,
from my own street
and from the Andean frontier. . .
    The Times-Herald, Manitowoc, Wisconsin:
    ''. . . The people of America want peace.
    Let them have it.''
             Arthur Trippler

do you hear us?

Walter Lowenfels

RETREAT

Oh we marched to the tap of that
musical extravaganza, the hip Jews
and Italians in the band, the sun almost
down, the company commanders smiling
past the stand filled with wives and
officers, guests of the dead, the
honored.
            From their bright American mouths
the syllables articulated over the dense
blatancy of the band, dress right you motherfuckers.

past the stand, the grass soft, in spring, or
bitter hard in winter under the weight of
overcoats and rifles, the feet sweating

in their boots, we marched to that
tap of music, the drums swollen out on the air,

the dead honored, the living holding their
medals under the guidons of the battalion,

the guests a continuous blur, khaki
and pinks, and the womanly pink or yellow,

a face weeping, broken in pain, the hands
around the black leather box with

the Silver Star inside, the corpse
of some sergeant deep in the endless snows

above Ko-no-ri, dead and rotten
for a rotten fabrication, a bad job,

a fuckup as the troopers say, it
was not worth it, the guilty killed and
the innocent, the vicious and the gentle,

ignorant men destroyed by
large pieces of red hot medal.

We marched then out into the roads
with no sound but the hiss of leather/and clump.

young men and so many with old old faces.

Gilbert Sorrentino

I KNOW I'M NOT SUFFICIENTLY OBSCURE

I know I'm not sufficiently obscure
to please the critics--nor devious enough.
Imagery escapes me.
I cannot find those mild and gracious words
to clothe the carnage.
Blood is blood and murder's murder.
What's a lavender word for lynch?
Come, you pale poets, wan, refined and dreamy:
here is a black woman working out her guts
in a white man's kitchen
for little money and no glory.
How should I tell that story?
There is a black boy, blacker still from death,
face down in the cold Korean mud.
Come on with your effervescent jive
explain to him why he ain't alive.
Reword our specific discontent
into some plaintive melody,
a little whine, a little whimper,
not too much--and no rebellion!
God, no! Rebellion's much too corny.
You deal with finer feelings,
very subtle--an autumn leaf
hanging from a tree--I see a body!

Ray Durem

STRANGERS ESTRANGED

Strangers in a strange land
By whose hand
Were you brought here
Kabyles at Chapelle and on the docks at Javel
Men from the heat of Tunis
Under a leaking roof in Grenelle
outcasts of the colonies
now our coolies
little suns shining in grey mornings
now in our land made free to be
scavengers for all the filth of Paris
knackers of beasts already dead
Gypsies at the outer gates
Polacks in the fogs of Marais
Children of Senegal
brought here to work
thrown out of work
Strangers estranged
Strangers estranged
Fishermen from Mallorca
shoemakers from Cordoba
Franco's scapegoats
deported since the Spanish war
to Paris and Navarre
the liberty they fought for
was our own
by us disowned
Black slaves of Frejus
hunted down and chained
beside the sea they bathed in
Black slaves of Frejus
at evening in our workhouse
echo the birds of their forests
on a wire-strung cigarbox
Strangers estranged

Children of Vietnam
acrobats and jugglers
their harmless knives impounded
strolled the cafe terraces
to sell their pretty paper dragons
Children grown too soon and too soon gone
Today you sleep face down
in your homeland's earth
While your ricefields
are tilled by bombs
That's your pay
for your folded paper dragons
and we let you have your knives again
in your backs.

(1951)

Jacques Prevert

Adapted from the French by **Teo Savory**

ENGAGEMENT AT THE SALT FORK

Like tumbleweeds before the wind we moved
across the continent's huge heedless face.
Fat sheriffs' radios kept hot with news
of our invasion. Squad-cars tailed the walk.
Blasts born on Yukon tundras knifed us through
and buffeted our sign: *MAN WILL END WAR
OR WAR WILL END MAN.* Handful that we were,
armed men patrolled us, secret agents sped
ahead to warn the elevator towns.
Christians heard now that if they harbored us
and let us spread our sleeping-bags on floors
of Sunday schools, religion would be lost.
Whoever opened up his door to us
was spotted by a telephoto lens,
proclaimed suspect, anathema to all
right-thinking patriots. As if we were
the ghosts of banished Cherokees come back,
the guilty Strip shook in its cowboy boots.
We camped one night beside the Salt Fork, near
a town through which they'd hustled us with guns
and imprecations lest ideas start
an epidemic there. Our campfire lit,
potatoes boiling and someone's guitar
strumming *Down by the Riverside*, people
began to drift in from the country round.
Skylarking students with a bugle, torches,
burlesquing us with signs: *Workers Arise!
You Have Nothing to Lose but Your Thirst! Drink Beer!*
Good kids they proved to be and soon knocked off
the clowning. Faces in the firelight grew
into hundreds, boys with their dates, big-hats
from nearby ranches, preachers whose wives had brought
us popcorn, apples. A dozen arguments
swirled into being as good-humoredly
they challenged us to win their minds with fact
and logic. Raw through the night, shirt-sleeved they stood

and battled with us till they came to see
the meaning of our walk. Some would have joined
had we sought that. One horse-breeder, Stetsoned
and powerful of frame, told of campaigns
he'd fought in Italy. Fondling his son,
a lad of eight, he blessed our walk for peace.
"Each war *we* fight, *they* promise is the last,"
he said, "and here they go ag'in. This boy
is one they ain't a-goin' to git, by God!"
Long after midnight it was when the last
of them went home. I could not sleep for pride
in these my people, still square-shooters, still
ready to tote fair with the other man.
I could not sleep for sadness too, to think
how these great hearts are gulled with lies.
God help the liars when my people wake!

John Beecher

On the San Francisco to Moscow Walk for Peace, 1961

FORT DIX, 1961

One deer.
Seventy-five men
Wearing khaki and steel,
Two weeks without women.
Silence on the machinegun ridge.
The sergeant volunteered a deadly finger.
The deer edged to the forest.
You know the rest.

Arthur Dobrin

JUNE THROUGH SEPTEMBER , 1963

I
A quiet summer for Private Harry Barclay
    he fell clutching olive earth
    olive clad—
part of the mud of another land

II
While passing the Mount McGregor Home
    for mentally deficient children
late at night only three lights touch
    the road
from that mountain where a boy
strikes his head against the wall
and will not stop
I think of him
the radio is loud
the valley and the road are rain and leaves
I point toward light and voices

III
    On June 11
old Thich Quang Duc
    crosslegged and calm
    sat on the warm asphalt
    and touched the match
that flowed his saffron robes
from gold to charcoal black

IV
A Dragon Lady hisses gently
    "Do you know how long it takes
    to become a Buddhist monk?"
the lessons are learned quickly
ten more play phoenix for their faith

V
A colored kid who threw a rock
got blasted off his bike
and in a church
the blood of four young children
lends color to *our* hands
the face of Christ
was blown clear out
of one big stained glass window
perhaps the face filled in now
will be black. . .

. . .Ajax Telamoniades
deceived by the Gods
disgrace then darkness
came over his eyes
on the plains of Troy
a giant falling on the sword
that smote his enemies in battle
and purged his shame
while burning through
the twisted hidden guts
that we deny.

Joseph Bruchac

BURN UNIT

The eyes of the child
are chrysanthemums
crumbling into the
heart of a flame.
The cheeks, chalk pale,
are dry moon craters.
The mouth is blurred,
a line of blood
smeared by a finger.
The hair is a frame
about a photograph
of a battlefield
innocent as the grass.

This head, an obscure bust
is forever witness
to a landscape of
cloth and flesh
melted together
darker than Delta soil.
To breathe, to eat,
to move, these
are miracles.
But sweat is a curse
and tears, for
the body's salt
sears like the first fire.

The identity tag
a perfect silver planet
hovers above the chest
and reflects
your face.

Joseph Bruchac

THE CHILDREN COME

The children have come from Phuong Boi

The stone house is ready the Delaware
River flows by speckled with coins of ice
the pumpkins have turned and been
cut Candles within show their mouth and their eyes
apples are russet for bobbing The tow-heads
are noisy at play The two darker ones silent
and still Their more delicate hands are folded

The children have come from Phuong Boi

When they came from Suchow and Amoy
it was summer Grain was tucked into
sheaves We danced in the barn Fiddles squeaked
lanterns blackened their chimneys Hunt the slipper
came at the end and that ended with prizes
Theirs had been stamped: Made in Japan They
stamped them into the floor then sat in silence

The children have come from Phuong Boi

Once they came to the house by the Wye
There was snow and their clothes were too
thin The bonfire lit up their thin cockney
faces They shouted at sight of the Guy
burning bright as a city Their country cousins
made fun of their voices till the Guy
went up in the sky in a tall flat-topped cloud

The children have come from Phuong Boi

When they came from the towns in Japan
some gave money at sight of their skin
Never more Never more but now they've come
once again and two women for making a
protest are locked in a cell They spend three
nights with four other women all of them black
who say they've got children themselves at home

The children have come from Phuong Boi

Teo Savory

49

TWO CHILDREN

I: Admission

Burning, the child runs down the cobbled street,
into the lens, along the quivering wires,
onto the front page of this evening's **Times**,
and to my hand, which just this morning signed
the tax return.

Now ink spots metamorphose, blue to red,
as burning flesh leaps hours and continents
to scald my fingers, render indelible
stains that swell and throb to make me know:
this hand that held the pen should clench instead
on prison bars.

I hear a cry: startled, I raise my head--
surely that burning voice could never reach me
all the way from Vietnam. The cry
comes once again.
 I breathe, recognizing
my youngest calling, ready for his bath.

II: Ablution

Begin, small son, with your face:
why is it splattered with mud?
 (Mud, thank God, not blood;
 before the hour of our Judgement,
 what will you have to face?)

Here now, behind your ears
and inside each curving hollow--
 (Hear now, what sound will follow?
 Is that the sputter of sparrows?
 Pray not the singing of spears!)

Now for the baring of arms,
soap from shoulder to wrist.
    (May all your energy's risk
      spring for the trophy, the touchdown--
    never for bearing of arms.)

Scrub the marks from each hand,
wrist to knuckle to finger.
    (The marks of my love will linger,
      but useless as shield or shilling
      when the due-date is at hand.)

I'll help you wash your back,
lather along the spine.
    (God, such a vulnerable line:
      too frail for bandage or bondage
      if we are ever paid back--
      when we are ever paid back.)

Sally Buckner

ONLY YOU AND ONLY ME

''I would like to say one thing. This is mainly to the young people here, but really to everybody, and that is that ultimately you can listen to only one thing, and this is not your President, not your many misguided leaders, save a few, and not the Communists or the Socialists or the Republicans or the Democrats. But you must listen to your own heart, and do what it dictates. Because your heart is the only thing which can tell you what is right and what is wrong. And after you have found out what you think is right and what is wrong, then you must know that you can say yes to what is right and no to what is wrong. And that you young men, for instance, if you feel that to kill is wrong and to go to war is wrong, you have to say no to the draft. And if you young ladies think it is wrong to kill, and war is wrong, you can say yes to the young men who say no to the draft. Because it is not the leaders and the dictators, it is not God who is going to get us out of the bloody mess we are in. It is only you and me.''

Joan Baez

SANE Emergency Rally on Vietnam
Madison Square Garden
June 8, 1965

Regina DeCormier-Shekerjian

1966

I

Pax
Pox
How do you spell
the word that was spoken?

Pax
said the Pope
and the earth trembled
beneath the genuflecting
weight of pious thousands.

Pax o Pax
intoned the Pope
and the earth shuddered
beneath the holy weight
of twice-blessed thousands.

Pax o Pox o Pax
cried a representative
of the Pope
and the earth received
the napalmed murdered flesh
of Vietnam's thousands.

II

Broken
deranged, in sleep
I am no longer sleeping.
I dream
and all my dreams
are burning burning   who
is burning who who
I call down all the streets
echoing endless doorless
in dreaming lit
only with burning. In sleep
I am no longer sleeping.

I dream
and all my dreams
are faces, children's
faces, fire-
flowered vaselined flystuck
faces hiding
brown-paper-bagged faces
burning burning endlessly
burning, their screams
knifing
the night, and me
deranged, dividing
dreams into Ns of continuous
dying; writing
reality in sleep, I am no longer
sleeping and shame
despair intolerable
grief have blackened the sun
of day.

Regina DeCormier-Shekerjian

POLITICAL PROMISE

Dust with smoke rises up thick from the burning village huts.
Confused victims scatter towards the shallows of the river and
swim frantically in the shelled water. The wounded lash about in
the bloodied current. One frightened boy has his hands over his
eyes and does not bother to fight back the tears. Another kid is
hiding behind the trunk of a huge tree. Army men look by at the
choking peasant girls, and their mother hovering in sudden
terror with her baby shielded in her lap.

They wonder what next
when a flame-thrower is the beginning. They see the fire raging
up through their thatched security and stored rice. They realize
in the terrible moment that their bodies had been flushed out of
their ancestral homes like wild game. And for some political
promise worked out over lobster and champagne music and
tropical cocktail whores.

Art Cuelho

MY COUNTRY

This is my country,
between these fingers
runs the rivers of my land.
I stand here on the banks of my knuckles.
Here I defend the backs of my hands.

This is my country,
deep in these cracked palms
springs the source of my creation.
I swim here in the depths of my blood.
Here I know my duty to the wildflower.

Art Cuelho

A VOTE FOR PEACE

At 21, a tree and an inlet
point him north.
One home he has left behind,
the other is joined to a hope
from which he swings
toward any road
a fair wind blows
to a book by a fire
or a song in his hand,
and a smile sealed in a letter
under his pillow.
What stars there are
he willingly shares
with those at sea,
in the air,
or trapped in foxholes.
He camps alone.
Time fills his bones
when night comes.

Elizabeth Bartlett
*This was written for a draftee who refused to fight
in Vietnam and went to look for a peaceful life in Canada.*

SAY NO TO THE SELECTIVE SERVICE SYSTEM

R.F.D #1 Box 197B
Voluntown, Connecticut
February 25, 1966

Local Board No. 125
Norfolk County
60 Adams Street
Milton, Mass. 02187

Gentleman:

On June 5, 1964, I was registered for the draft under the Selective Service System. Since that time, I have seen the government of the United States rain bombs upon the people of Vietnam. I have seen American soldiers burn the homes of Vietnamese peasants with cigarette lighters, with flame-throwers, and with napalm bombs. I have seen the government of the United States lie to the American people and invade the Dominican Republic. I have seen thousands of American troops enter battle against the people of the Dominican Republic on behalf of their oppressors. Moreover, I have repeatedly heard spokesmen of our government threaten to wage total war — nuclear war — against the people of the Soviet Union and China.

These actions of our government are crimes under the Constitution of the United States; they are crimes under the Charter of the United Nations, and under international law; and, most importantly, they are crimes against humanity. In attempting to act as the world's policeman, this country has made itself an outlaw.

I refuse to participate in these crimes, and I declare my intention to do all that I can, as one citizen, to stop my government from behaving in this manner.

Thus, I have chosen to discontinue my participation in the Selective Service System, an essential part of this nation's war machine. I have destroyed the draft card that I received in the mail today and have also destroyed the Registration Certificate and the Notice of Classification that you sent me previously. No longer will I cooperate with the Selective Service System or any part of the military apparatus. I choose this course of action because I think it is the duty of every American to say "NO" to the government and to face jail rather than fight in a brutal war of aggression against the people of Vietnam, the Dominican Republic, or any other nation.

David Allen Reed

SEARCH AND DESTROY

They faced each other
ticking as time present — time bombs
at equidistant points of amazement.
Tin men, two men, time men.

Was it for this they had been created,
I thought, for one to kill, one to die.
Was it for this they had been created.

I felt I was there!
Said to the taller, "Don't shoot! don't shoot!"
Time up. BANG! He did.
The flash riveted time to the other
like a clock unwound.

Johnny Baranski

FOR PEACE

convicted,
that stigma
like a meathook
snagged the scruff
of my neck
and flung me
on a grill,
flames leaping
all about,
to the sting
of captivity,
its clamp
of steel,
the smell
of brimstone,
a taste
of ash.

Johnny Baranski

THE DESERTER

Mr President
I pen you a line
that perhaps you'll read
if you can find the time
Today in the mail
my induction notice came
I must leave for the war
Wednesday night or before
Mr President
I won't do it
I'm not on this earth
to kill other people
Don't get angry
I've got to tell you
my mind's made up:
I'll be a deserter

Since I was born
I've seen my father die
I've seen my brothers go
and their children cry
I've seen my mother suffering
because she was still living
while some fed the bombs
and others fed the worms
Now I'll be robbed of my wife
I'll be robbed of my soul
and my precious past life
But tomorrow morning early
I'll shut my door
and go on the road

I'll beg my bread
on the highways of my country
from one boundary to another
and I'll tell everyone I meet
Don't do it
Refuse the draft
Don't go to war
Refuse it

If you want to give blood
Mr President
then give your own

And if you try to catch me
warn your henchmen
they can safely shoot me:
I won't be armed

Boris Vian/Teo Savory

WOMEN STRIKE FOR PEACE

We arrived at the Washington Monument, five busloads from New York, several from New Jersey, a group from San Francisco. In the vastness of that park, which I had seen crowded only once, in August of 1963, it looked like a tiny gathering. A few more buses pulled in, and the number grew. The rally began.

Amy Swerdlow spoke and then the mother of Ronald Lockman, with news that her son, a soldier who refused to go to Vietnam, is in good health in a California military prison, and that six of his buddies are joining him in the protest. Mrs. Doris Turner of the Drug and Hospital Workers Union made the connection between the Vietnam war and racism here. Gary Rader, blond and boyish, turned the Jewish mothers on with a direct appeal for love and nourishment. Francis Rocks, a Vietnam veteran, whose change of heart came in the angst of combat, read nervously a stilted little speech like a high school valedictory that was the more moving because the punctuation was so precise and the "g's" were missing. And then Dagmar Wilson, undisputed Queen of WSP, described her visit to Hanoi and invited us to "follow me."

We followed her. We had been given mimeographed instructions which suggested we chant a slogan as we walked: "Should they go? We say no. We back the boys who will not go."

For several blocks nobody chanted. The usual conversation ran through the crowd, guesses as to the size of the turn-out. One young girl wanted to run up to the front of the line and count. The new demonstrators always are thrilled at the size of a crowd, always notice that the faces of the people in the line are soft or sweet, so different from those of the cops and hecklers. The old demonstrators wait quietly, perhaps screwing up the courage to chant once again, to put themselves on display so loudly in the streets. To me this is always the hardest part. I resent the forces we are opposing all the more for putting me to this insignificant discomfort of doing something so foreign to my urban upbringing. In other words, I can never get over feeling like a fool, shouting in the street, and my shouts, whatever they profess to say, are a wail of flesh, a sacrifice to the gods of stupidity that rule this earth. Every slogan is a curse, after all.

An old woman muttered behind me, "We're supposed to be chanting." And she began, and we in front of her took it up half-heartedly. From the beginning of the line we heard our words echo, louder and more enthusiastically. We envied their effort and tried harder. Nobody was there to hear us but a few passersby and the people in their cars along the avenue. And then we came to our first destination, the Selective Service Headquarters, where a delegation of women had an appointment later to give General Hershey a dressing down. Across the street from the building, a couple of women held up a black coffin with the words, "not ours, not yours, not theirs. Stop the war now."

On a grassy slope next to the General's office sat a group of young hippies who answered our chant with "Hell no, we won't go." The marchers applauded the kids, the kids applauded the marchers. We circled the street once and then followed Dagmar on to the White House.

Now the word was passed along: "Walk fast approaching Pennsylvania Avenue. They might try to cut us off." And every time the police stopped the line for traffic, we broke into a run to fill the gap.

We knew that the Department of the Interior had made a ruling that no more than 100 people could march in front of the White House. The women had been in constant negotiations with the powers to revoke the order and we fully expected it would not be enforced. The President of Italy was visiting the White House. Surely Johnson would not embarrass himself by setting the police on a delegation of mammas!

But there they were, helmeted and ready for riot duty. They let a hundred or so women across, and then they stood, their thick boots planted in the ground like so many steel posts. We were incredulous. We looked at each other, mothers, grandmothers, little children. What would they do to us if we went through? Up until the actual encounter with the cops I think we all really expected them just to step aside when it became clear we were determined to pass. I remembered when Kennedy served coffee to some marchers on a winter day, the courteousness of the Washington police during the Jobs and Freedom demonstration, the way one Easter they good-humoredly let a radical peace group break their line and stomp up the Capitol steps; on another peace walk a woman sat down by the White House fence to nurse her baby, and children climbed on the gates.

Women Strike for Peace does not ordinarily indulge in civil disobedience. Most of the women have families depending on them. Kids waited at home with sitters. A day off is one thing; a night or two in jail or the hospital quite another. And for many there on Wednesday it was not only their first antagonistic experience with the cops, but their first participation in a demonstration!

We, predominantly white middle-class women, were on the other side of the "riot" scene now. We saw the robot eyes of the fuzz and understood how the stance alone, the costume, the armor are in themselves adequate incitement to riot. Grimly ready, they waited for us to act. We argued about going through, most of us nagging each other, "What are we waiting for?" The rule of 100 in front of the White House was clearly a breach of the First Amendment. All along the march we had been promising "the boys who will not go" that we would back them up all the way. It seemed that we could not renege now. There were, also, future demonstrators for us to consider. If we did not challenge the ruling, what forces might challenge them? What new edict—the outlawing of all protests in Washington?

People went down the line warning the women that they might subject themselves to arrest if they pushed on. Someone suggested we wait for Dagmar to come back and get us.

Then, suddenly, the crush started. I felt women pressing at my back; women backing up against me from the front. I had a terrible fear of being trampled to death, a fear not unfamiliar to a New Yorker. I grabbed a hand on either side of me, to make sure somebody in the world remembered I was here. I moved forward. I saw nightsticks crash as the police line gave way under our pressure. I found an opening and ran through.

On the ground lay the casualties, and a half-dozen policemen were pounding the living hell out of Gary Rader and Francis Rocks. Maybe it was the cops' chance to redeem their self-image. Young men are more respectable prey than women, even if they're unarmed.

We were on the other side of the street, a few feet from the lucky hundred. Again a phalanx of cops, pushing and hitting. A blonde girl, about 20, stood on the curb with a baby girl in her arms. The cops were swinging wildly. We shouted to her to get away. She wouldn't move. We offered to take her baby back across the street to safety. She refused. "You don't understand," she said, "her father was killed in Vietnam."

I shouted something obscene like, "Don't make her die, too!" and then I cried in frustration and fear for the baby.

The women stopped beating at the cops. The cops stood their ground. The sacred sidewalk was safe for Lyndon Johnson and the DAR. We sat down in the road. From a squad car a loudspeaker announced that we had two minutes to go back or we were all under arrest. Nobody moved. Girls passed papers around for the signatures of those who wished to be bailed out.

The two minutes dragged out into ten. The singing began. Lorraine Gordon, with only a few hairs out of place in her Kenneth coif, held up Francis Rocks' tweed coat, ripped in three pieces. A woman shouted "'Shame!'" to the cops. Nobody made a move to arrest us.

Bella Abzug, formidable as her name, loomed through the crowd. She told us that the police had offered a compromise. We could all march in front of the White House, 100 at a time, if we first went back across the street. Shouts of "No!" She called it a victory.

Dagmar came through. She advised us to leave and return when we were better organized. Like any uncertain mob, we followed our leader. Dazed and dissatisfied, stumbling and cursing, we made it back across Pennsylvania Avenue. Where was the traffic? The street seemed wide, like a sea, or a battlefield. We waited on the opposite side for the word to go forward again. A cop tried to keep us moving. He began to shove, in the ordinary way of cops. I said insanely, "Don't you have any manners at all?" He put his hand down at his side and said, "Please ladies, move along."

Leah Fritz

WEAR SHOES

[*sign in a restaurant window*]

you have the right to protest dissent
if you exercise caution
who wants to be flabby
but not in public places not too loud
no vulgarity not too often
be a gentleman a lady a eunuch if you like
of course you have the right to ask for
          a redress of grievances
certainly but not in a state of undress wear shoes
don't be unreasonable ungrateful uninhibited
                    a traitor
if you must dissent do it in private
          in your home try the bathroom
don't look like bushmen come out of the jungle
          wear shoes
carry an attache case with dignity
you never know
you may not have a heart attack until you're fifty
if you can't look like a business man smell like one
jolie eau de toilette in different sizes
be congenial compatible compassionate toward
          animals never kick them when wearing shoes
          but wear shoes
and no foul language
try the language of diplomacy euphemism
it's so convenient for making war
          propping up dictatorships
              reviving tired politicians
                  building concentration camps
wear shoes

Mary Engel

I was a clerk in the District Attorney's office when plans were made by the LAPD to deal with the peace demonstrators who planned to gather outside the Plaza Century Hotel, where President Johnson was to appear...

JUNE TWENTY THIRD IN THE CITY OF THE ANGELS IN THE YEAR OF OUR LORD ONE THOUSAND NINE HUNDRED AND SIXTY SEVEN...

I

Upstaged
By the smooth
smooth architectured
20th century facade,
the joyful fountains
danced
their topaz ballet
here within
the theatre
in the round
where there were
no wings, but lines
of marchers —
and the strings
inside the theatre's pit
beneath the Plaza's floor
were bars —
constructed overnight
by Fear
and state employees.

II

But did you hear the music of Freddie Martin's band?
Come—Recall the music of Freddie Martin's band.

III

What was on the menu?
Was it pheasant under glass?
Those who read the press reports
might know it.
Were there conversations
that the censors could not pass
were there documentaries
to show it
do the documentaries describe
the fountain's play. Did
you hear the screaming
just a club away?

What was that, Walt Whitman, turning in your grave.
What was that, we thought we heard you say?

IV

See the Flower Children weeping
and the orange fountains leaping
and the stark white helmets keeping
Order of the Day. . . . . .

"Stop beating her, you bastard!
Are you crazy! Are you crazy!
That's a woman! And a baby!
Not the children! Not the children!
We *can't* back any further
There are cops that block the way!"

Saigon — June 23 (Released through A.P. June 24 — done day late "for security
reasons")
"An American Infantry Company — caught in a deadly crossfire. . . lost. . .
Seventy-five killed. . . twenty-five wounded. . ."

Why
do they
call it
The Infantry,
Dr. Spock?

V

The old soldiers have not died
The old commitment makers have not died
The old munitions makers have not died

VI

"Kosygin and I agree
that we want
a world of Peace
for our grandchildren"

VII

See Dick
See Jane
See the Aeroplane
See Jane jump
See Dick die
See the aeroplane
with the bomb turrets
on the hellish
fiery fountain
in the theatre
in the round
where all the wings
are broken
and all the clubs
have spoken
where all the strings
inside the theatre's pit
beneath the Plaza's floor
are bars. . . . . .

VIII

There was a pitcher bleeding in the plasma colored fountain
and the voice of the multitude was rising in the mountain

IX

But did you hear the music of Freddie Martin's band
The anachronistic music of Freddie Martin's band?

Sadie Wernick Hurwitz

AND DOVES WERE NOWHERE TO BE FOUND

More bombs & planes/than birds & clouds
flew in skies   Suns & Moons had retired from.

Doves were nowhere to be found.
& flowerchildren searched for broken wings.

And it was then that the world came to me   & said
in a voice i could easily understand   /in tears
it spoke:

Help. help.

And i turned to the wind   who had also spoke in tears
And through eyes which had long since given up looking
i looked again   /for one last time
& again i saw   as i had seen before
:Tears on the faces of broken dolls.
:Reflections of bombs in the eyes of children.

And in a voice which had long since given up shouting
to ears & minds which had long since given up listening/
i softly answered:

Help. help.

Jesus Papoleto Melendez

CACAPHONY IN STATE PARK CAMPGROUND

CAW   CAW   CAW
taweet   taweet   weetweetweet
bidda biddarum

How fortunate we
who can communicate
by words and music
all the arts,
by touching
one another.

With all these ways
to relate. . .
            Why do we still use
            bombs and burnings
            rapes and shootouts
            wars
            which give one message only:
            our inability to communicate.

CAW   CAW   CAW
taweet   taweet   taweet
bidda biddarum

Janet Carncross Chandler

THE GARDEN GATE

Mutilated bodies,
Three
   of
      them,
Lie grotesquely beneath
        the
      garden gate.
No faces, no feet,
No manhood, ever to be felt again.
Why?
The people ask,
        Why are they here?
An old man,
Obviously lying,
Claims the Americans killed them.
Naively an open-faced lieutenant says
        Never!
Americans couldn't,
        No absolutely never!
Later he was proved wrong.

Peter Berenbak

THE GAME

Wanting to cry out in anger!
At the racism so
Blatantly accepted as
Part of our daily existance.
Black
       As well as
            White
Skillfully play the game.
Blacks just learning;
Whites practicing for home.
Gook,
      Dink,
         Slope.
Colorful words for a
Less than human race.
The stage is now set
For the triumphant third act.
Kill them all.
Everything!
Since they're not really people
It can't be murder,
But an act of revenge
For intruding on our
once well ordered world.

Peter Berenbak

WAS THIS ALL THERE WAS TO SEE

Oh where,
        Oh where
Did they all come from?
Whores, whores and finally,
Till I could stand it no more,
Still more whores, at almost every door.
Oh where,
        Oh where,
Did they all come from?
Coke girls,
        Bar girls,
                Pubescent pimps,
Scattered like poppies
        Row upon row,
As far as the weary eye can see.
Waifish shoeshine boys boldly
Offer the willing GI the finest smack—
And then, for good measure, they steal your watch.
Oh where,
        Oh where,
Did they all come from?
Steam job,
        Blow bath,
    "We massage everything,"
The signboard loudly proclaims.
Was this all there was to see?
"Hey soldier!"
An unctuous Indian shopkeeper,
Beckons a passing GI,
"Dollar numba one,
                Communism numba ten.
Change money?
Best deal around!"
Was this all there was to see?
She stands on a corner,
Deaf,
    dumb,
        mute,
            And scarred,
Pitifully offering herself to anyone.
For less than a dollar.
But no one seems willing to meet the expense.
Was she all there was to see?
Attention everyone!
The Americans proudly proclaim,
We've come to save you—
To help the people, help themselves.
But somewhere a voice is heard to ask—
Save them from what?

74   **Peter Berenbak**

AMERICA HURRAH!
Regina DeCormier-Shekerjian

THE INDUCTEES ON THE PLANE
1968

They sleep on, in the seat next to me,
And our elbows touch
While the plane plows toward Saigon.
I look at those medals
On their chests—Maltese crosses
Like the ones the Nazis wore—
The heavy crosses of men in graves,
Men who have taken their defeat.
And yet these are the faces of Flemish
Girls in paintings, and faces called for,
Those years that mothers did the wash
And heard the politicians tell them
What to buy.

When they wake we talk about the war
And I'm all hemmed in, one to my right
And one to my left.
They don't get angry, they wait
For the significant
Battle to begin, not just these words.
We all know how it ends, and when it does
We'll stand in the streets
And not bother to put our helmets on.
High school football told us how.

So then I take their cigarette.
Why face them with the right
Or the wrong of it? Why profane
Their sacrifice, invade their privacy,
Churn this heavenly journey into mud?
We sail through clouds that dance.
We're cherubs. We're cute. We're
Little sunbeams of Jesus.
Their act is made in good faith
Like a bad marriage, and they're off
To fuck the bride.

David Ray

AN EVENT IN ASIA AND SHAKER HEIGHTS

In an isolated event
Somewhere in Asia,
A boy twenty
Steps on a mine
And is instantly killed.

This sets in motion
A chain
That ends at the door
Of an apartment
In Shaker Heights,
Where an embarrassed soldier
Dressed in green
Must tell
A tremble-chinned lady
Gray curls flattened
To her head
With the man
Half bald behind her,
That all the years
Of care
For this human being
Carried under her heart,
Through childhood
To adult
Have been obliterated.

Laurel Spear

PERSONAL END OF A WAR

I think my brain stopped when I read the words
because there was nothing in my head--
nothing--
and you know my thoughts
have always been like birds in an aviary
flying all ways in color;
it had all closed down to a gray silence.
Then you took the letter from me
and touched my arm
and a Roman candle went up inside me
and I remembered from the beginning:
a fat baby
a happy boy
a young man like you young again,
a young man with a heart like a sounding guitar.

They said he was a hero.
Do you think a hero in the family
is better than a living son?

Margaret Flanagan Eicher

CADAVER 1467

Today at the Gateway
to the Pacific
Travis AFB California
we loaded a cattle
truck full with
bodies fresh off
the plane from Con Thien.

Vacuum sealed in
smooth extrustions as
shiny and neat
as your latest poptop
beer can:

> **Container, Cadaver**
> **Aluminum, PROS 1467, Reusable**
>
> **Nomenclature of Contents**
> **The human remains of**
> **Transportation #757XOD3967**
> **Cpl   E4**
>
> (or some kind
> of sergeant once
> that weighed 143 lbs. net.)

Tarp over to protect
motorists from the glare
on the highway
to Oakland the truck
pulled out and we watched
silent
        wiping wet palms
on our green thighs.

Tom V. Schmidt

Chuck Logan

NURSERY RHYME

I am the shell that awaits the word.

I am the gun that fires the shell
That shocks the solid flesh so well.

I am the hand that pulls the cord
(Now more potent than the sword)
When that certain word is roared.

I am the voice that roars that word
That touches off the deadly bird
When ordered by the one who's heard
From those who say it's time to gird.

I am the one who teaches to read
Those who spread the ancient creed
To aid the ones who feed the need
Of the hand that's forced to heed
The word that fathers forth the deed.

I am the one who works the drill,
Who tills the soil, who takes his pill,
Who backs with tax the shell he makes
To feed the hand of him who takes
The word that comes from certain men
Who give the word to fire when.

Who is this one who gives the word
To lift aloft the deadly bird?

I am the one behind the shell
I am the one who makes this hell.

Leo Hamalian

NEW VISION

I saw God one day in a vision
of a dirty old panhandler
who clutched the sleeve
of my clean coat with his dirty hands
and said, "Got a quarter for a beer, buddy?"
His vacant mouth was a wide grin.
I jerked away, brushing
the remnants of his touch
from my sleeve
I looked quickly over my shoulder
at him
and he was watching me, laughing.

Another time I saw God
in a beautiful broad with ten children.
She came to me in despair for help.
And I gave her words of wisdom.
when she left she laid her hand on mine
and said,
"You are like God."
But she didn't know that she was like God,
and that I wanted her.

And once I held a child,
black and unwanted,
and as the dirty hungry arms
closed around my neck,
I shivered at the alien thing against me—
the touch of God—
that I have forgotten now.

For I don't see   God anymore
because I am a proud member
of the trained dominant race of conquerors.
I wear medals on my uniform
that prove I am a liberator
bringing the war of peace.
God is the salve of my conscience
and my weapon is my might.
Prayer makes me righteous
to prove my power
as I walk among men,
feeling their obeisance
to my goodness.

Now I know God again because
I am God.

Brother Bernard

RESOLUTION

You fight us
because we fight hatred
while you feed on hate and violence
for strength.

You curse us
because
we don't give man a label
and turn a gun barrel on him.

You condemn us
because you can't use our blood
in paying off your debts of avarice and greed,
because you can't budge us
from man's side
where we stand to protect all life.

And
you murder us
just because we bow our heads
before man's love
and reason.

Because steadfastly
we refuse to identify him
with
the wolves.

Thich Nhat Hanh

RECOMMENDATION

Promise me this day,
promise me now
while the sun is overhead
exactly at the zenith,
promise me.

Even as they
strike you down
with a mountain of hate and violence,
even as they
step on your life and crush it
like a worm,
even as they dismember, disembowel you,
remember, brother,
remember
man is not our enemy.

Just your pity,
just your hate
are invincible, limitless, unconditional.
Hatred will never let you face
the beast in man.

And one day
when you face this beast alone,
with your courage intact, your eyes kind,
untroubled
(even as no one sees them),
out of your smile
will bloom a flower
and those who love you
will behold you
across ten thousand worlds of birth and dying.

Alone again
I'll go on with head bent
but knowing the immortality of love.
And on the long, rough road
both sun and moon will shine,
lightening my steps.

Thich Nhat Hanh

READY TO FIGHT, READY TO DIE

I

alloyed clown
malable copper poet
why a sensible stamp of approval
from the govt. to write what you think.
are you ready to die?
for what cause?
for what?
it's been pounded into mind:
shape up or ship out.

. . . rat-a-tat-tat
hands knotted in war
you bitch pen, bastard sword
infuriated, in love?
Why match m-16
with the will to obey or fight or even die?
look out, man, dodge those bullets.

II

Poll reveals. . .
man seeks understanding
is basically an aggressor
likes to be allamerican
and fight in viet war
like that.

read all about it in boston globe editorial:
number one first lieutenant
man made hero machine
found ambushed in vietnam—
body sent home for presidential unit citation
the whole bit.

some joke
the emptiness left after war
nothing but sheer and a relearning of why
your fingers formed V for peace
in a causeless medallion war,
that vision of bomb children
beside human ashes;
tiny skulls gone up in smoke.
brutal, those plastic explosive remains.

III
it's funny coming down off
therapy this time
an alloyed clown
copper malable poet
and a somewhat tarnished tin soldier.

Preston H. Hood III

THE BALLAD OF BASIC TRAINING

''What is the spirit of the bayonet?''
The sergeant's shout commands.
''To kill'' is the ancient answer
The sergeant's shout demands.

The words seem so ineffable
To ears unused to sounds
That come from sergeants' frenzied mouths
And rifles' frenzied rounds.

The hesitation makes him rage
And so the punishment--
Heavy guns held in hurting arms--
For our astonishment.

Until the voices grow so loud
The training field resounds:
''TO KILL!'' ''TO KILL!'' the arms repeat
In military rounds.

One voice merely mouths the phrase
Wondering how it happens
That laws of letters are twisted
Till words become weapons.

Even the boisterous barracks boys
Are quiet all that night
For shouted words whisper to them
The fate of those who fight.

Although not skilled in definitions
They wanted no explaining,
For learning what a word can mean
Is very basic training.

Alan C. Lupack

ARMY EXPERIENCE

I was a Black man
sold into slavery
herded from my native land
hoarded for my value
not as a man
bound with chains
into a servitude of soul.

Now that I've learned their dark white ways
they send me weak and wanting
into the world.

Does the strength return,
my Black brothers,
before the soul despairs?

Like you,
I know the hurt
and the hate,
but not how many centuries
it takes to be free.

Alan C. Lupack

A NEGRO SOLDIER'S VIET NAM DIARY

The day he discovered a mother and child in the river, he wrote:

They had been there a month; the water had begun to tear them apart.
The mother had not relaxed, even in death she held to her child.
I lowered my gun slowly into the water, walked away.
My stomach screamed empty, there was nothing there.
What little warm water I had would not Pilot away the mud or stench.
It was like a dead body we could not discover.
Death hangs on the rice.
The ground is watered with blood.
The land bears no fruit.
Grass is an amenity.
It is a luxury forever to notice so much as a flower,
Or clear water in a stream.
Bullets, here, kill with the same deliberate speed that they do at home.
Fear destroys the thing it is unacquainted with.
I never want to kill again.
Do not celebrate me when and if I come home.
I step around the smallest creature these days.
I am cautious to pray.
I am cautious to believe the day will come when we can
Take up our sharing again with deliberate speed.
Have you prayed, lately, for that?

Herbert Woodward Martin

ONUS 2

Our onus: you own us.
Your surplus usurps us.
Your justice adjusts us.

    All this, to preserve your status,
    Which you thrust at us
    And say trust that it's
    For our sustenance.

You frustrate our every refusal
To diffuse us and confuse us.
Your business:
To keep us busy
Being used to being used.

    But your custom made suits don't suit our customs.
    Your gusto turns into our disgust.
    So realize: We are only on loan —
    And over due.
    The onus will soon be
    On you.

Bob Feldman

CON/S/PIRACY

Attention privates!
This is your general speaking.
You have been b/r/ought here
To be sold/iers.
You are s/killed workers
And must be (al)armed.
We are (de)faced with a grave situation.
The (mi)stakes are high:
We must (def)end all subversive activities.
I expect you to accomplish this (o)mission
For(get) our government.
Do your (de)part now.
We need to be (up)rising to(day,) our call.

Bob Feldman

"Ma," he took a deep breath and gulped, placed his knife and fork across the plate, brought his elbows up to the table, rested his chin where his clasped hands formed the bottom of a large, inverted V, and said, "I may not be going to Vietnam."

After a pause that seemed longer than it was, his mother stood and peered down at him. "What?" There was tension in her voice.

"I might not go tonight. I've been thinking about it for weeks and. . ." He stopped in mid-sentence, his stomach rumbled, and he resisted the urge to leave the kitchen.

"You're serious?"

"I think maybe I should go to Canada, and decide what I'll do from there."

"But son," she said nothing else, and waited for her only child to respond, to ease the confusion in her mind. He said nothing.

"What will your father say?"

Looking down at the yellow-streaked plate the young man answered in a weary voice, "Isn't it time for it to matter what I say? What I think? What I feel?" He clenched his teeth. "Mother, I am not at all sure this war is right. I think maybe those people marching and demonstrating make more sense than the people I am in the Army with."

She looked at him, stunned. "Is that reason enough?"

"Mother, please, don't make me have to go through this twice." He stood and looked out the small window over the kitchen sink.

In a low voice, almost inaudible, the woman muttered, "I can't believe this," and went into her bedroom, closing the door behind her.

Matthew went into the backyard and thought of his father coming home. Would he be able to explain that posters that said *What if there was a war and nobody came?* made sense to him? What would the older man think if he knew that his son thought that when the young women dropped the daisies down soldiers' rifle barrels it was a touching act? If he decided to go to Canada how could he explain his transformation from loyal son to deserter? He decided he wouldn't: he would still be a loyal son, but he might not have a loyal father. He became anxious thinking about his father's arrival and went inside.

"You don't want to go to Vietnam." The ease and softness with which the words were said belied the seated man's appearance. He shook his head as if in disbelief or wonderment, then looked over at his wife who sat statuelike. He stood and yelled, "you don't want to go!" As impulsively as he stood, he again sat down and took a drink from his martini.

"You have to go. You have orders to go—it's not like deciding where you want to take a vacation." As he spoke his voice became less excited. "What did you do, get drunk last night and decide you'd rather get laid in Sweden instead of kill gooks?" He forced a grin. "It's really very simple Matt: you enlisted in the Army and now must do what you are told." He sounded like a teacher talking down to a student he knew he could intimidate.

"Dad, I am not at all sure about the war, or just wars, or even about the military anymore. I do know that I have feelings, and emotions, and a conscience, and that all these things are telling me to question my life." The young man waited until their eyes met. "It's not 'all very simple'."

"Get me another drink, Jean." He was taking command. "And you, get in here and sit down."

He had been a good son, filling most of the rolls expected of him. Marriage would come eventually, and then maybe another Matthew Hayes. They didn't talk about that either. Big Matt fought in the big war, and big Matt's father, Tom, fought in Ireland.

"Why Matt, what's making you say this? I know you're not afraid." An image of his son, years past, skating down the side of a hockey rink, stick chest-high, eyes frenzied, flashed into his mind. "And what of your future—you would be a coward for the rest of your life if you didn't go." As he spoke he looked at his son's stockinged feet; the son watched his father's lowered eyelids. The bigger man continued. "It's not like us Mattie, it's just not us to walk away! The Army never did me any harm. Don't you believe in your country?" His face reddened, accenting the veins of his neck.

The son drew small quantities of dirt from beneath his fingernails by gliding them through a small gap between two of his bottom teeth as his father spoke. His mother remained motionless on the other side of the couch looking blankly, like an observed bird, as each man spoke. Anger saturated the air; as the men talked the realization that no matter what the younger man decided, the relationship between father and son as it had existed would be irrevocably transformed was evident to both men.

The older man stopped talking and raised his eyes to his son's indicating he wanted answers to his questions.

"Dad," he spoke softly and slowly, "I still might go," he paused, "but if I don't, it will have nothing to do with cowardice. It simply doesn't make sense to me to fight in a war I don't understand. And please," he glanced at the magazine-strewn coffee table to the side of his father's chair, "don't give me any bullshit from *Time* or *Newsweek*." He looked to his right, "Sorry for swearing ma."

"Don't understand! You took an oath didn't you? Weren't you sworn in as a soldier in the Army? And what about the men you've been serving with?" Something would hit home.

"Yea, I took an oath, but it didn't say for me to get my brains blown out for no reason. And I know that some of the guys I'm in with are the best I'll ever meet — and they have no doubts at all about going to Vietnam. I respect them, and I hope that if I don't go they won't think less of me." He rubbed the sweat from the palm of his left hand into the arm of the couch.

A stillness filled the room. None of the people's mouths moved, giving their faces looks of grim determination. Finally the mood was broken as Mr. Hayes reached for and finished off in a gulp his second drink.

"Look son," his voice was calm, "we have never really let each other down. Never. Later on, when you come out of your bedroom, I want you to be in uniform. Then we'll go to the airport—I know what you're going to decide." He rubbed a hankerchief across the back of his perspiring neck, then cast a glance at his wife expressing something she had not seen in years. His eyes seemed to say *we're going to do it babe—everything is going to be o.k.*

As passengers passed them on their way to the embarkation point for Chicago, Matthew, his mother, and his father stood in awkward silence.

Matthew stiffened as his father came within a half step of him. The mens' eyes met and the smaller man held back an impulse to flinch when his father raised his hands in the air. His palms came down on his son's shoulders and his face went ceilingward in emotion as he jerked what he felt as extensions of his flesh and blood to him and wrapped his arms like a loving mother around the soldier. "Go, Mattie." He pressed his chin into his son's shoulder and closed his eyes, "don't even think about it, just go."

Matthew drew back his moist face from against the warm material of his father's jacket. Bewildered, he looked beyond his father's forlorn stare to his mother. She nodded her head quickly, unseen by her husband, and allowed a fleeting smile.

After a handshake and a kiss the wan soldier turned, then walked through a canvas tunnel leading into the airplane.

As the plane ascended from the ground, rising as if it were being pulled skyward by an awesome, unspeakably powerful magnet, the young man looked out the small window. The earth became more patterned, more precisely laid out as the plane surged upward. Horizontal patches of green were bordered by fields of other shades of green. The wide, straight swath of highway upheld cars, trucks, and buses which looked like distant toys scurrying from one bound territory to the next. The plane held at the same altitude as he looked and saw the mosaic of straight, sometimes crossing lines separating farmlands, towns, wooded areas, and water. The lines were railway tracks, and roads, and long slashes of great web-like highways, and borders, and established boundaries. The turnpikes were fed by avenues, which were offshoots of streets, which had alleys and driveways penetrating them. The aqua paint of empty swimming pools and tennis courts that looked like fallen dominos identified one part of a city as much as a dense concentration of high, black rooftops, and an absence of green did another.

His country was no longer an abstraction he could not grasp. This was America: a land owned, already controlled, already parceled out, already spoiled, already figured out to such an nth degree that its children could be sent to die or be maimed halfway around the world because an idiotic progression of events had mushroomed from an initial mistake to a national disgrace and the same men responsible for dividing the land below did not have the courage, or sense, or honor, or humility to stop it. Although only they had the power to do so.

Honor, democracy, an American way of life were words to fill school children's heads as they grew into citizenry to take their places within the confines of the divided land as unthinking, unquestioning adults.

Soaring again the plane leveled off as wisps of small clouds, like suspended, oversized puffs of smoke, their existance as fragile as a fountain's spray, passed the plane's windows like the visible breaths of heavenly ghosts.

"Good evening, sir." The stewardess beamed at the soldier. "Will you be going on to San Francisco from Chicago?" she asked automatically.

The soldier looked up with the meek expression of someone entering a crowded room with a black eye. The stewardess smiled at him. "It's not as bad as all that, is it?" She kept smiling.

He loosened his tie and replied, "No mam." He cleared his throat. "At O'Hare I'm going to change my ticket to Vancouver—that is allowed isn't it?"

"Yes sir, it is. Would you like to order a cocktail?"

"You know, I was about to order a scotch and soda—a double in fact." A bead of sweat evaporated on the back of his neck. "But never mind that. I think I'll just have a cup of tea instead." The stewardess marked his request, nodded, and ducked into the next trio of seats. Hayes removed his shoes, pushed his seat back, and began thinking of life in Canada.

William Powers

TIM

I understand that you just decided to become a C.O. when your plane landed in-country.

It's something I've been thinking about, sir.

You mean you're not going to carry a gun while you're in Vietnam?

That's right, lieutenant.

I understand you're facing a court-martial.

That's right, sir.

Doesn't that concern you?

Not as much as killing somebody for no reason whatsoever, sir.

Isn't this a little late to be changing your mind?

Have you ever heard of continuing revelation, sir?

Do you play bridge, Specialist Hertz?

Yes sir.

We need a fourth in our office, I'll see what we can do.

Sandy Primm

THE PEACE OF GOD

"Christ, what was that? Where's the bunkers, sounds like
we're getting hit," the new man screams as he jumps out
of his chair.

"It's Happy. Don't worry. Have a seat. Would you like
a beer?" John asks.

"But that was mortars, wasn't it? Incoming?"

"It's just the Happy Mortarer. Every afternoon at four
he shells the hill outside the base."

"That's crazy, there's nothing there." The man was
still frantic, but he took his seat to listen.

"Whenever he does it, our artillery just blows up the
mountain right behind Happy."

"But he might drop a few in here."

"Happy wouldn't want to hurt us. Someone would have
to go after him if he did. So, he keeps mortaring the hillside."

"Oh," the new man pauses, "I see."

"Do you want a beer?"

Sandy Primm

RADICALIZATION

"Stop it," the First Sergeant yelled. Kept me waiting in his
office for an hour or more then the XO came in with the Colonel.
The only reason I wasn't being sent to the infantry, they said,
was that I had only a month left in country.

After that I looked around before drawing peace symbols.

Sandy Primm

94

KOREA, 1968
For a brother fighting in Vietnam

The morning of the G.I. is here
Tall and straight, cold and clear
A Korean winter, I read Stars and Stripes
It is John's death I fear.

K.I.A. — last column last page
Each day I seek escape from naming,
From body counts, their maiming
For my days are owned by others. . .

And the rules of those who die within a hush
In a single conspiratorial rush, the blind
Ants afloat the tide, possessed, so small
Wash ashore asleep the sullen mouthing crest;

With one last wish farflung mothers blow the kiss
Of lotus blossoms that fall on the ocean's hem,
That flutter and unfurl in ribbons of stars
But the best young men can only faintly mutter
Facedown in the petals and the dung.

Andrew Glenn

UPON HEARING MY UNCLE'S WAR STORIES FROM WORLD WAR II

Bombs!
Bombs!
What maddening beasts,
How they burst and buck
Rear their roaring heads in thirst,
Sucking sugar,
Sucking sugar from the mouth of pain.

Shame!
Shame!
Uncle Joe,
Your flying stallions of the Ruhr
Have manes that flow red with flame,
What a show!
What a show!

Bombs!
Bombs!
What hellish hail,
People burst and buck writhe and flail,
Melting on soft shouldered streets in single file
Where war is strength
That cannot fail,
Where women cannot smile.

Uncle, Uncle stop the rain!
Where is hope
Where is shame
We are stealing sugar
From the mouth
Of pain.

Andrew Glenn

War Is Hell!
Ask The Man Who
Fought One
VIET-NAM VETS
BRING
GIs
HOME
ALIVE!

from I DON'T WANT TO TALK ABOUT IT

Like the princess in the fairy tale
it gets hard core, you're
the property, the prize
your father the King gives away
to the warrior
who wins
the fight
> like war and sex
> like men and women
> in our Kingdom, follow
> the same order, domination
> and submission, like war
> over the land, like war
> over the women,
> the spoils, the prize, what's
> taken
Like the 4000 member
CIA Killer Squad
Like plastic pellet bombs
that cannot penetrate
steel or rubber, only
human flesh, geared
to explode
at the height of the average Vietnamese

war is about our sex, war is the hatred
of the body, like
napalm, the fleshfire
that can't be put out
> like the 22 year old woman
> you force water down
> then jump on her belly, you, the whole
> squadron. You capture her 3 times.
> 3 times she escapes. Rests.
> Comes back to the front, now
her misshapen body, her heels
you shaved off, the finger you plucked.
The color of her skin
is not a color. But you
are in her body now,
the fits she has
wherever she goes, what
you did to her
she repeats over and over
what you don't want to remember
> *You can do anything to me.*
> *I'll never talk. Free*
> *my country.*

Sharon Doubiago

I drive the valiant blue Valiant
to the bereft and bereave them
I say:

Dear Sir or Madam or Mrs, it is my
sad duty to inform you that your
husband, son, brother, father (choice of one)
is dead missing in action marrying a Vietnamese
and beloved by all his comrades and commanders

(A. Ground) While on a sweep of the
Central Highlands, Saigon bars, DMZ he
threw himself on a whore grenade 1/Lt
thereby sparing his comrades or
(B. Air) Flying from the MPs, Thailand, Phu Cat
he machine gunned took pictures of sprayed
sixteen of the little bastards before
they got his young ass, rendering vital service
before he was rended

The body, head or other remains may be sent
to the local undertaker of your choice or
viewed at the nearest military installation
with his rank embroidered on it

Gratuities
            are not necessary

Horace Coleman

FEED ME

More war
More guns
More missiles, bombs and gases
(to purify the masses)
More dope
More booze
More radioactive shoes
Some diseases that crack stones
and dryrot your bones
—or is pollution the solution?—
More strikes   More freaks
More sniping in the streets
More lying   More spying
More suicides by frying
More wrecks   More duels
More masochistic fools
Hate now   Don't wait
Die young   Not late
(there'll be no ripple for your stone
and I'll be happy all alone
so save a breath for death
that's me
your friend
I'll see you soon again)

Horace Coleman

SATURDAY RIP-OFF BLUES

When seeing what was happening on fourth and main
fearless johnson yells fear not I'll help/and being
a man of his word and because he just like sticking
his nose in things that have no concern of his he
sends 500,000 with orders to stop whatever it is
that's happening there but not too fast for he wants
to make a profit also/in runs a man with a flag in
his hand and stars on his eyes take me he yells I
want to stop whatever it is we're supposed to stop
this time/sam hits him with a mother and some pie
which transforms him into a handsome harry every
mother's son he runs off and does the job and when
he gets back the pride he once felt for the job is
dead and he runs off looking for johnson and
sam law and police makers at large. This goes on for
about 54,000 life times and no one tries to stop it/
now crazy johnson seeing that all that can be gotten,
has, splits fast with all he can carry leaving the mess
for someone else to clean up/everyone is running around
fourth and main saying they will do the job of clean
up but none of them mean it for to get everything clean
would put them out of jobs on both sides/plump hubert
mumbles something and walks away/while in sterile sub-
urban tracts they have song birds chained to the tops
of telephone poles which sing out when someone cracks
a whip/and children are trained to hunt them with
bee-bee guns, but the children don't know why they
are trained to hunt and kill/they will though when
they are 20 and sent to fourth and main/when in runs
dick from the coast he says he can do it while he
helps tie and gag this black man in chicago/what did you do
before now asks weird willie of hopkinsville of dick,
why? says dick no reason says willie just thought i'd
ask i heard you sold cars once and you would sell your
mother if it would bring a profit/willie is bound and
beaten by men from madison avenue with f.b.i. tattooed
on their foreheads and they throw willie into a cell
for the duration and 6/dick wins and in seeing what he
has won he says we want peace but let's not lose face
we must change but not too fast, etc./which if broken
down says i'm going to get mine too just like johnson/
anyone want to buy a used car?

Steven Hassna

101

MY LAI

WHITE LIFE MAGAZINE photograph rocks out
the weekly hit parade/marquee blinking it's
two children it's real
draped across the road like mangled screams
choking the earth
with small limbs.

Descend the furious tunnel
of burns that singe off eyelids,
shrieks that shred the eardrums.

The blood spurts from wounds
like hydrants.
The bells cough up blood all night.
A fist beats the breath
to a pile of webs.

Six year old brother fell,
a muddy shudder in the road.
Six more years and he would reach manhood.
At twelve in Vietnam one has seen the world.
One has speared beasts in the night
approaching like lengths of ice and hunger.
Ten year old brother
dropped beside him
before the guns and
curled out an arm
as if to protect them from all harm.

The blood wells up in unbearable pools.

Defoliants
Made in the USA.
Women are giving birth to monsters.

Against the scarred windows
near the empty table and chairs
rust sets in like snow.

Doug Yamamoto

from IF ASIANS HAVE BEEN QUIET

radio voice asks one brother
"is it true that Asians
as a whole, etc.
have been quiet about the War?"

"yes, that is true."

six eyes cut through cement
like a flurry of comets

bullshit if Asians been quiet

if Asians been quiet
tell me if the sound of that man's tears
as he walks through the countryside of Viet Nam
& that Asian woman on the podium
before the people
tells the story of a mother
forced to watch her baby
die by her torturers?

if Asians been silent
explain the coalitions & the rallys
describe the meetings & the arrests
the soul-wrenching grief
& iron determination
for a final victory
yet to be

if Asians been silent
why do loudspeakers vomit
on the yard
"Lee 1970
Moriyama 790
Oba 9757
Sumida 11977
Yamamoto 10364
These men have visits."

three men turn off the radio
and get ready for Count

voices link up with voices
deep from the bottom
of a great groundswell
comes a people's chant
rattling their chains
& shaking the world

Doug Yamamoto

CALLEY AND THAT OLD BITTERNESS

When the United States Court of Military Appeals recently upheld the conviction of William L. Calley Jr. for the murder of at least 22 Vietnamese civilians at My Lai, my old bitterness and disgust were stirred.

My background was very similiar to his. I was a drifter of sorts before I enlisted in the Army in April, 1968. I was looking to find myself, or whatever it is that an eighteen-year-old looks for when he leaves home for the first time.

Soon after I joined, the Army offered to send me to Officer Candidate School because the loss of so many junior officers in Vietnam had forced it to lower the standards of admission. I accepted because it was the most challenging thing the Army had to offer me, and I figured that if nothing else the Army could teach me to be a man. I graduated as a second lieutenant at the ripe old age of 19.

The Army has a rather peculiar way of teaching prospective officers the qualities of leadership. If a person can tolerate being treated as the lowest form of life on earth, being subjected to incredibly sophomoric and often sadistic forms of discipline, and being told that nothing he does could ever possibly be correct, then somehow after six months this qualifies him to lead men into battle.

The reason for all this, they say, is to teach men to think under pressure. But this method doesn't teach how to think, it teaches how to obey—blindly and unquestioningly. In addition, many candidates get the mistaken impression that this is how to run their own platoons, which accounted for, I think, so many lieutenants in Vietnam dying from gunshot wounds in their backs or grenades under their bunks.

We had to try to reconcile this obedience with another crucial lesson. Everything in Officer Candidate School is against the rules, so a candidate soon learns that rules must be broken for things to get done—a handy tip for the future in Vietnam. The only rule that was always followed was this: Don't get caught. It was a big game; senior officers would obligingly look the other way if we showed "ingenuity," but if we were too blatant we would be "caught." Lieutenant Calley got caught.

The court rejected his appeal that he was only following orders when dozens of villagers were shot in March, 1968. I cannot defend him for what he did, but I can understand the circumstances under which it happened. I never participated in any so-called atrocity while I was in Vietnam but that was only a coincidence of time and circumstance. I could have—I had been trained for it.

The only guide that confused young men like Lieutenant Calley and me had in Vietnam was morality, and the Army had done its best to eliminate such a defective idea. If you do not disobey an unlawful order, you get into trouble, but all orders are considered lawful unless you can prove otherwise, usually at your own court-martial. Nobody seems to have pointed out that the Army probably would have been more willing to try Lieutenant Calley for *not* killing those people.

Lieutenant Calley was foolish, but so were we all. How can we isolate and punish instances of criminality in a war that was totally criminal? Where is the logic of sending one man to jail for killing civilians with bullets and making heroes of others for killing civilians with bombs? Of course, that is the way of our society. Those who give the orders are never punished; only those who get caught obeying them are allowed to be crucified.

Peter P. Mahoney

TO MY YOUNGER BROTHER

You were wide-eyed at the manhood
Pinned above my pocket
I saw the pride and the hunger
I felt the pulse in your veins

Must I break your fragile innocence
With my sledge-hammer guilt?
How shall I endure your why
Slashing like a razor to my wrists?

Yet you must know
Or learn as I have,
War does not make men
It destroys them

Peter P. Mahoney

MAU THAN

A Poem at Tet for To Lai Chanh

1.
Friend, the Old Man that was last year
has had his teeth kicked in; in tears
he spat back blood and bone, and died.
Pielike, the moon has carved the skies
a year's worth to the eve. It is Tet
as I sit musing at your doorstep,
as the yellowed leaves scratch and clutter.
The garden you dug and plotted
before they drafted you is now
stony, dry, and wanting a trowel.
"For my wife," you said, taking a plum,
but the day never came nor will it come
to bring your bride from Saigon.
Still the boats fetch stone, painted eyes on
their prows, plowing the banana-green river;
and neighbor children splash and shiver
where junks wait to unload their rock.
But shutters locked, the door of your house is locked.

2.
A year it was of barbarities
each heaped on the other like stones
on a man stoned to death.
One counts the ears on the GI's belt.
Market meats come wrapped in wrappers
displaying Viet Cong disemboweled.
Cries come scattering like shot.
You heard them and I heard them.
The blessed unmaimed may have too.
So many go stumping about.
The night you left I turned off Hoa Binh
and saw a mined jeep, the charred family.
A Vietnamese cop minded the wreckage;
his gold buck teeth were shining
in a smile like a bright brass whistle.
Can you tell me how the Americans,
officers and men, on the night of
the mortaring, in the retching hospital,
could snap flash photos of the girl whose
vagina was gouged out by mortar fragments:
One day we followed in a cortege
of mourners, among the mourners, slowly walking,
hearing the clop of the monk's knocking stick.

3.
If there were peace, this river would be
a peaceful place. Here at your door
thoughts arrive like rainwater, dotting,
overspreading a dry, porous rock.
In a feathery drizzle, a man and wife
are fishing the river. The sidling waves
slap at her oar as she ladles the water
and fixes the boat with bored precision.
His taut wrists fling whirring weights;
the flying net swallows a circle of fish.
His ear wears a raindrop like a jewel.
Here at evening one might be as quiet
as the rain blowing faintly off
the eaves of a rice boat sliding home.
Coming to this evening
after a rain, I found a buff bird
perched in the silver-green branches
of a water-shedding spruce. It was
perched like a peaceful thought. Then
I thought of the Book of Luke and, indeed,
of the nobleman who began a sojourn
to find a kingdom and return.

4
Out of the night, wounded
with the gibbering of dogs,
wheezing with the squeaks of rats,
out of the night, its belly split
by jet whine and mortar blast,
scissored by the claws of children,
street sleepers, ripping their way free
from cocoons of mosquito netting
to flee the rupturing bursts
and the air dancing with razors
--out, I came, to safe heaven.
Nor looked, nor asked further.
Who would? What more? I said.
I said: Feed and bathe me.
In Japan I climbed Mt. Hiei in midwinter.
The deer snuffled my mittens.
The monkeys came to beg.
I met Moses meeting God in the clouds.
The cold wind cleared my soul.
The mountain was hidden in mist. Friend,
I am back to gather the blood in a cup.

John Balaban

BATTLE NEWS

For breakfast — war and coffee. Pilots
have been downed like skeet, and captives
tortured in a tub or booted in the groin
until they talked. A Cardinal approves
of troop morale. His speech before

the V.F.W. is reproduced beneath
the photo of a sergeant burned in error.
After three wars, I should be numb
to every morning's muster of the dead.
The Cardinal seems numb enough. He preached

a twin address the year I swore
to fight all foreign and domestic
enemies with nothing but my hands, so help
me God. When I marched home, I might
have told his Eminence, ''Don't

talk pluralities to me. I breathe
alone and so do you, and one
times one was never more than one.
The smallest pin of pain can show
that one umtillionth of the world

is not the name that anybody answers to.''
I never breathed a word, and now the daily
deathcount booked between the weather
and the baseball scores leaves nothing new
to say. The cost remains numerical,

the order, alphabetical. Only the spellings
change from war to war. Between
the lines I think of aborigines
who would not touch their wives or eat
until they had atoned for every

enemy they speared in battle. Justice
or no justice, shall no one say
that hunters rove the earth from now
to heaven? Who cares if men in diving
suits are swimming to the moon like sperm?

They're out for battlefields where flying
armies shall dispute the stars. I know
it's militarily absurd to claim that life
means more than trying not to die,
but if it does, what then? What now?

Samuel Hazo

from THE DARK NIGHT OF RESISTANCE

We have taken up, one after another, almost every question except the one which would liberate us: the question of man. How is a man to live today? How is he to live; is it possible for a man to do something other than kill his brother — the practical universal demand laid upon him by the state, approved by a silent Church?

Since the times are dark and uncertain (I will be going to jail, as sure as tomorrow. It is as though a man were to awaken one morning with the bitter revelation on his tongue — I am going to die. I am going to jail. Like a man with terminal illness whose cunning apothecary has come on a new potion, I am spared a few days. The days are here. But I live under proviso. That is my freedom and my urgency).

Let the communities who have carved on the keystone of their monasteries PAX learn what some of us have paid dearly and known for long: There's a war on; can you smell death? Do you know what peacemaking is costing us? Where are all those good things you purportedly hold in escrow and never share with us? Have you ever attended one of our political trials, seen us dragged off, read the cheap price put on our lives and deaths by the frosty eye of power?

To save the earth and those who dwell upon the earth and those who love and tend the earth, and those who inherit the earth and bequeath the earth to children, and those who contemplate the earth and draw upon its energies and beauty and surprise; in order to make poetry, in order to make love, in order to make sense. It may be necessary to go under the earth. To go underground. To join that vast network of the unborn and the dead. To resign from America, in order to join the heart of man.

Daniel Berrigan

NOTE FROM THE UNDERGROUND

After four years of resisting war, and many more years of resisting exploitation, misery and racism, we had taken thought among ourselves. Our conclusion: it was better to burn papers than to burn children. . . For the (draft board) papers destroyed at Catonsville in May of 1968 were in fact hunting licenses issued against human beings, licenses declaring a twelve-month open season on Vietnamese men, women and children.

Daniel Berrigan

from THE TRIAL OF THE CATONSVILLE NINE

And so we stretch out our hands
to our brothers throughout the world
We who are priests to our fellow priests
All of us who act against the law
turn to the poor of the world   to the Vietnamese
to the victims   to the soldiers who kill and die
for the wrong reasons for no reason at all
because they were so ordered by the authorities
of that public order which is in effect
a massive institutionalized disorder
We say: killing is disorder
life and gentleness and community and unselfishness
is the only order we recognize
For the sake of that order
we risk our liberty   our good name
The time is past when good men may be silent
when obedience
can segregate men from public risk
when the poor can die without defense
How many indeed must die

before our voices are heard
how many must be tortured dislocated
starved maddened?
How long must the world's resources
be raped in the service of legalized murder?
When at what point will you say no to this war?
We have chosen to say
with the gift of our liberty
if necessary our lives:
the violence stops here
the death stops here
the suppression of the truth stops here
this war stops here
Redeem the times!
The times are inexpressibly evil
Christians pay conscious   indeed religious tribute
to Caesar and Mars
They pay lip service to Christ
and military service to the powers of death
And yet   and yet   the times are inexhaustibly good
solaced by the courage and hope of many
The truth rules   Christ is not forsaken
In a time of death some men
the resisters   those who preach and embrace the truth
such men overcome death
their lives are bathed in the light of the resurrection
the truth has set them free
In the jaws of death
they proclaim their love of the brethren
We think of such men
in the world   in our nation   in the churches
and the stone in our breast is dissolved
we take heart once more

Daniel Berrigan

NEWS

1954

While the French army sunk into red muck
like a smashed wine cellar at Dien Bien Phu
(and German paratroops in the foreign legion
crumpled in the rubble, wearing Nazi belt buckles
emblazoned "GOTT MIT UNS")
an eight year old boy in Lehigh,
Pennsylvania, carefully cut out the war pictures
from the Sunday newspapers and *Life* magazine
and tacked them on his bedroom wall
beside tiny crossed U.S. and Confederate flags
(souvenirs of Gettysburg) and a U.S. Air Force
official glossy photograph of a B-29 bomber
in flight, courtesy of a recruitment sergeant
in Scranton.

Ten years passed, rumors of another round of war
greeted the graduates of high school that year.
The handsome, grinning, crew-cut athlete
who accepted his diploma with a whoop
in the center of his class glanced about
the mined-out ridges of Lackawanna County
and the drab half mile of "downtown" Lehigh
driving home after the graduation party,
and decided to join the marines and see the world.

1968

"The long range artillery pinning the marines
for days that stretch into weeks at Khe Sanh
drives some men insane, like the sergeant
from somewhere in Pennsylvania who ran alongside
each outgoing stretcher case being raced
to often doomed choppers and cargo planes
bracketed by Vietnamese fire—and greeted
replacements dashing out of the aircraft
with a bellow: "Welcome, idiots,
to Dien Bien Phu II'." (wire service dispatch)

When it came time to send him home

there wasn't enough left to fill a casket.
The family decided to have no epitaph
carved on the grave marker;
his mother, red-eyed, remarking to a reporter:
"I don't know. . . What did he die for?"

1969
Some college students at Penn State
took the name from the casualty lists
and put it on a poster which a young woman
carried in a long line with the others
from Arlington National Cemetery across the Potomac,
across Washington, to the steps of Congress
one long night under a guttering candle:

> WILLIAM R. WEAVER
> Lehigh, Pa.
> Dead In Vietnam

A photograph of that white placard
held just under the young woman's chalk white face
in the dark passing the silent White House
went out on one of the wire services
and was published in the *Stars & Stripes*,
from which it was carefully torn out and tacked
on a wall of a bunker near the Cambodian border.
Beside it hung a hand-carved peace symbol on a thong
and a button from a stateside correspondent
of one of the soldiers, emblazoned:
"Make wine, not war."

Jan Barry

LETTER FROM NAM

for my brother, Verne

On June 10, 1969
eight days ago
you were alive.

Your hand
moved across these pages.

Your flesh was intact
your young heart
was beating,
there was life
in your body
on June 10.

> We who sit and wait
> pull the minutes apart
> between newscasts
> the daily death toll
> and letters.

Eight days ago
you wore a helmet
with a peace sign
sprouting flowers.
You posed for this
polaroid with two
Vietnamese children
the three of you
calling time out
to send me a sign
of peace, their
chubby fingers
recording this
day in history
June 10, 1969.

S. Lee

EXHORTATION

Today
5000 miles across the waters
the face of a boy
who was to answer
one of my songs
was peeled away from the skull;

    Now my words
  (I do not know which)
     will never find an anwer.

   MY SON!
      MY SON!
shattered mirror of my longing

15 years ago in a rice field
the dark heart of a man
whose blue verse
I was to answer
was burnt & blown away;

    Now my response
    wanders unjustified
    & lost
    in the labyrinth of my blood.

How many of my fellow priests
are silenced?
We are killing our dreams;
our words are orphaned.

My country, what madness
have you suffered
that our hearts are bleached?

The angels no longer walk among us;
our household gods have fled;
we have lost records
of our shamans' graves.

Think you can survive
making the trees naked?
(There are spirits in them
more power than your guns.)

Think the rice will bleed
without a scream?

You cannot shatter the mirror
of your brother's face
& hope to live.

Beware, my people—
    do not forget to kneel
Beware, my people—
    the joints of the heart ossify
Beware, my people—
    do not dare to address the gods
    with unholy fire

BEWARE MY PEOPLE

My countrymen, listen:

My mirror has already turned
obsidian
to sacrifice my masks.

Take heed:

The mirrors of the country
will soon refuse to give us
back our image.

Rafael Jesus Gonzalez

FOR TIMOTHY CLOVER

Few know a death's precise day and hour and minute,
the knowledge that freezes sundials.

One froze
at 1:28 A.M. on the 22nd of May 1968 in Vietnam
when Timothy, soldier, poet, husband, father was shot
dead. Heaven cannot hold all of him:

Scraps
of paper, unfinished poems found in his pockets,
float unseen on every wind, float
on in all their immense weight. . .
Sometime Timothy's bullet-holed, blood-
soaked pieces of poetry must weigh as much on this nation
as body counts of our nameless men.

I met you, Timothy,
when David read your poems, Davy, your good buddy, your
pallbearer and troubador who reads you back to life.
All who listen see your vision focus in Vietnamese
landscapes: mountains made crooked under napalmed
caps, laughter gouged out of children, women whose
bodies are joyless as mortar, ''that whirlybirdman
. . . colliding with a butterfly. . . ''.

Weep. . .
for what Timothy told is buried in the dreams-turned
nightmare of a generation of innocent G.I.'s who know
him in their scarred sleep.

My country's soldiers, I see
you rise in the West, assembled at the port that shipped
you out. I see you march, a funeral procession for Timothy,
march until you crumble every power at the wheels that drive
this war and stoke the next.

In the wake
grow sweet fields of timothy grass.
                    Rest In Peace.

Liz Farrell

CASUALTY LIST

At Fanwood, a few more commuters boarded, among them a young man with a neat square beard, wearing an army surplus fatigue jacket and carrying a clipboard. A small black-lettered sign hung suspended from his neck—End the War. He stationed himself at the head of the car and announced in a flat voice: I will now read the names of the men from New Jersey who have died in Vietnam. Eyes riveted on the clipboard, he began: Dunikovski, Walter E.; Pellicana, Joseph; Schneider, Stanley; Harris, Albert J.; Kohler, Robert A.; and on and on while Miller wondered how many in New Jersey; he made a rough guess, then multiplied by forty-eight, then by fifty, fifty states now—hit a figure—above ground burial in a ventilated crypt would require the Empire State Building, suitably renovated—Burchko, John H.; Moore, Reginald; Walsh, Robert—Miller listened only for Jewish names then remembered McQuaid, that goddam tabula rasa of a kid; he grew ashamed and heard all the names, all the names—Kelly, Michael; Noonan, John. He began responding after the names were called out: he'd repeat Noonan, John; then hurry to repeat the next one, Phillips, Daniel; Buckles, James. He'd repeat the names and hold them and remember them, cherish them, each one, each name, each name that disappeared so quickly, only to be replaced by another name, and on and on, names, names, names—and still the names went on—

Lester Goldberg

from TO STAY ALIVE

Chuck Matthei
travels the country
            a harbinger.
(He's 20. His golden beard was pulled and clipped
            by a Wyoming sheriff, but no doubt has grown
                        again
            though he can't grow knocked-out teeth.
            He wears sneakers even in winter,
                to avoid animal-hide; etc.)
And on his journeying bears
my poem 'A man'
to prisoners in the jails.
                Of Mitch I wrote it,
                even before anyone heard
                the voice he

118

                    brought to song
                    But Chuck has found in it
        a message for all who resist war,
                    disdain to kill,
                    try to equate
                    'human' with 'humane'
        (And if his intransigence
        brings us another despair
        and we call it 'another form of aggression,'
        don't we confess—
                    wishing he had a sense of humor—
        our own extremity?)

        'Living a life' the poem begins.
        '—the beauty of deep lines
        dug in your cheeks'
                    and ends,
        'you pick out
        your own song from the uproar.

        line by line,
        and at last throw back
        your head and sing it.'
                    Next on the mimeograph follows:
        **'THERE IS ONLY AS MUCH PEACE AS THERE ARE
        PEACEFUL PEOPLE'**
                    (A. J. Muste)
                    Then Chuck has written:
        This your only life—live it well!

        No one man can bring about a social change—
                    but each man's life is a whole and necessary part of his
                    society,
                    a necessary step in any change,
        and a powerful example of the possibility of life
                    for others.

        Let all of our words and our actions speak the possibility of
                    peace and cooperation between men.
        Too long have we used the excuse:
                    'I believe in peace, but that other man does not—when
                    he lays down his arms, then I will follow.'

                    Which of us deserves to wait to be the last good man
                    on earth; how long will we wait if all of us wait?

        Let each man begin a one-man revolution of peace and
                    mutual aid—so that there is at least that much peace. . .
                    a beginning;. . .

                                                            119

A beginning.
Where shall we
begin?
Can't go
further.
      Time, says the old Canon,
in Denis Saurat's *Death and the Dreamer*,
      is not a sequence,
      as man's simplicity thinks, but radiates
out from a center
      every direction,
      all
        dimensions
          (pulsations, as from living cells,
radiant —

May 14th, 1969—Berkeley
Went with some of my students to work in the People's
Park. There seemed to be plenty of digging and gardening
help so we decided, as Jeff had his truck available, to shovel
up the garbage that had been thrown into the west part of
the lot and take it out to the city dump.
      O happiness
      in the sun! Is it
      that simple, then,
      to live?
      —crazy rhythm of
      scooping up barehanded
      (all the shovels already in use)
      careless of filth and broken glass
      — scooping up garbage together
      poets and dreamers studying
      joy together, clearing
      refuse off the neglected, newly recognized,
humbly waiting ground, place, locus, of what could be our
New World even now, our revolution, one and one and
one and one together, black children swinging, green
guitars, that energy, that music, no one
        telling anyone what to do,
        everyone doing,
    each leaf of
    the new grass near us
    a new testament. . .

Out to the dump:
acres of garbage glitter and stink in wild sunlight, gulls
float and scream in the brilliant sky,
polluted waters bob and dazzle, we laugh, our arms ache,
                          we work together
shoving and kicking and scraping to empty our truckload
                              over the bank
even though we know
the irony of adding to the Bay fill, the System has us there—

but we love each other and return to the Park

Thursday, May 15th
At 6 a.m. the ominous zooming, war-sound, of helicopters
breaks into our sleep.

To the Park:
ringed with police,
Bulldozers have moved in.
Barely awake, the people—
those who had made for each other
a green place—
begin to gather at the corners.

Their tears fall on sidewalk cement.
The fence goes up, twice a man's height.
Everyone knows (yet no one yet
believes it) what all shall know
this day, and the days that follow:
now, the clubs, the gas,
bayonets, bullets. The War

comes home to us. . .

Denise Levertov

BERKELEY IN VIETNAM

The Hueys shrieked in low, so low I might have downed one with a well-aimed rock. But there were no rocks. Entering Sproul Plaza at the end of Telegraph Avenue, each spewed a yellow-green cloud, rising slightly to clear Sather Gate. . . A sea of high school classmates surged, parted like the tide.

And in the brief lull between Hueys came their screams. Blue-jacketed, helmeted, gas-masked billyclubs split heads and booted crotches, advancing in a robot-like phalanx. Khaki fixed bayonets cut off escape. Kids vomited; broke out in blisters; cried for water. . . Some clutched one another, keeping heads low. Others raised each other out of their own puke. An older handful hurled half-empty gas cannisters back at the clubs. And then more Hueys came. I could see no longer through the yellow-green curtains.

Prevailing winds protected us, the press, outside the cordon. "Jesus Christ!" a KRON cameraman muttered, squinting down. . . I held my rail, staring. These were my friends and classmates, the gentlest, brightest kids I knew. Kids from my art class, who'd volunteered to build a park, People's Park, on an unused, sunbaked lot.

Huey after Huey after Huey. Vietnam in Berkeley. In the TV's echo, counting Nixon's returns, I heard those radical leaders exhorting their victims to "Storm your Bastille! Seize your Harper's Ferry!" They'd appealed through bullhorns to ideals and glory, new Napoleons. Almost alone, I'd remained in class. I'd only heard the rifle-fire on Bloody Thursday, yesterday; only greeted the first limping survivors as they straggled back, not been among them. Club-swinging cops drove the rest like cattle. Then I'd joined the thick of it.

But before I did, I glanced backward at the crowd, my people, perhaps wrong but my own nonetheless. I glanced forward again, to 2,500 National Guard reinforcements spilling off trucks, clutching automatic rifles. I stepped through their forming lines to join my people.

I'd remained among them all the rest of the day, speaking to no one, taking notes. I'd helped block a Guard truck, kneeling before it with my empty Polaroid camera, forcing it to slam on brakes for me, a newsman, where it would have crushed the others. I'd lain on the ground, my body part of a vast peace-symbol, then of letters spelling 'love' and 'peace' to the Huey pilots.

In principle, I knew, my friends were wrong. One could not simply appropriate another's property, even 'public' property, even to build a park. But again. Ronald Reagan and the university regents were wrong for death, for building a laboratory on the park site in which to devise weapons and lethal chemicals, for sending the canvas-draped tanks and machine-guns arriving at the Berkeley Marina, when a fight had been the farthest thing from most of our minds.

Sunday we all marched, 50,000 strong, behind respectable, middle-aged churchmen now, who led half the town in mourning for the several dead and in protest against the violence, the provacateurs with their bullhorns at last justly ignored. From the flatlands past the park, through the hills, and back down we paraded, loudspeakers blaring Grace Slick, Bob Dylan, Janice Joplin, and Jimmy Hendrix. Girls choked Guard rifles with fresh bouquets. They were bouquets for the flower children, for the park-builders' own innocence.

The few people remaining gentle at heart spoke of leaving Berkeley soon, forever. The remainder grew grim with nightfall, the post-march street-dance and party becoming at once wake and war-dance, until the cops moved in again with the Guard behind. Now some of them were struck and injured. Now mayhem became rationalized, excused, used, and mutual. I'd watched this from a tree, sketching the silhouetted bloody revelers before their bonfires, with the eerie sensation that we'd regressed 4,000 years, that the violence was habit, that we would soon rip a virgin's heart out.

And still (years later) my brain reeled backward, to those concrete steps. I peered over the top while police dragged 300 of my classmates to waiting Black Marias. They were hauled to Santa Rita Prison; thrown into outdoor barbed-wire pens until parents bailed them out. Two girls I knew were gang-raped by Alameda County sheriff's deputies, men who might have been their fathers. One guy I knew caught the edge of a birdshot blast in the back. But I didn't see that. I only saw the Hueys, formation after formation. ''You're bombing your fucking children!'' a woman reporter screamed at them beside me.

She wept, shaking her fist; buried her head in my shoulder, expecting me to hold and comfort her. . . . I couldn't move.

Merritt Clifton

DIRGE FOR THE DEAD STUDENTS
Kent State University, Ohio, 1970

She'd only come to look
When bullets broke her flesh
A frosh, she held a book
 When bullets broke her flesh
 With almost wistful sighs
 Her face was round and fresh
With almost wistful sighs
The bullets raped her body
With almost wistful sighs
 They pierced her gentle body
 And her book dropped open to
 A page all torn and bloody
Her book dropped open to
A torn and bloody page
Containing nothing new
 A torn and bloody page
 Each child must learn to read
 A "History of Our Age"
Each child must learn to read
O study, students, study
This "History of Greed"
 O study, students, study
 Learn what they want from you
 Another age as bloody
Is what they want from you
Another age befouled
And nothing else will do
 Another age befouled
 By Great-Granddaddy's Greed
 (No wonder Ginsberg Howled!)
O Great-Granddaddy's Greed
Sucks, like a Vampire Bat,
The blood of his living seed
 Sucks, like a Vampire Bat
 The blood of our youth away
 Sucks, like a cornered rat,
The Pestilence of Our Day
And spits into our faces
The horrors of Our Day
 And spits into our faces
 Spreading disease and death
 That virus among the races
Spreading disease and death
Destruction throughout the world
With it's maddening murderous breath
 Destruction throughout the world
 That Malthusian explanation
 Picture the bombs being hurled
That Malthusian explanation
And a baby crying for shelter

While the Senate is on vacation
    And a baby crying for shelter
    And her mother and father dead
    And the bombs dropping helter-skelter
And her mother and father dead
And the President making decisions
(Who will his daughter wed?)
    And the President making decisions
    Search and Destroy is the way
    And the President making revisions
Destroy all their crops on the way
And the baby is blown to pieces
While the President goes to pray
    And the baby is blown to pieces
    While the President speaks to God
    And the rich collect rent on their leases
While the President speaks to God
And the students are shot for complaining
And the Haves of the world think it odd
    That the children (who Have) are complaining
    (These children have so much to learn!)
    And the government's busy explaining
For these children have so much to learn
In double-talk tripled twice over
How we keep what we get when we earn
    In double-talk tripled twice over
    How Ends do all Means justify
    In News-Speak all wrapped up in clover
How Ends do all Means justify
And death to the man who denies it
So, hush up, dear students, or die!
    For death comes to him who denies it
    As many dead children could tell
    And praise to the bastard who buys it
As many dead children could tell
And four dead students provided
A proof in the sun where they fell
    These four dead students provided
    Us all with a living example
    That day in the sun when they tried it
Gave us proof and a living example
Of what the "Great" in their greed are about
And four dead students are ample
    To show what the State is about
    (Christ, any one baby who died
    Should have left us no shadow of doubt!)
Now four young students have died
Shot dead in the name of the law
(But in fact for the lies they denied)
    SHOT DEAD IN THE NAME OF THE LAW
    FOR THE TERRIBLE TRUTH THAT THEY SAID

E.M. Schorb

WHERE DOES IT END?

The strife and fighting continue into the night.
The mechanical birds sound of death
As they buzz overhead spitting fire
Into the doomed towns where women and children
Run and hide in the bushes and ask why,
Why are we not left to live our own lives?

In the pastures, converted into battlefields,
The small metal pellets speed through the air,
Pausing occasionally to claim another victim.
A teenager from a small Ohio farm
Clutches his side in pain, and,
As he feels his life ebbing away,
He, too, asks why,
Why is he dying here, thousands of miles from home,
Giving his life for those who did not even ask for
        his help.

The War Without a Purpose marches on relentlessly,
Not stopping to mourn for it's dead,
Content to wait for it's end,
But all that the frightened parents who still have
        their sons hear is:
''the end is not in sight.''

Jeff Miller
Feb. 14, 1966

*Jeffrey Miller was one of the students killed by the National
Guard at Kent State University, May 4, 1970.*

126

KENT STATE

I was in Vietnam when I first heard about the thousands of people protesting the war in the streets of America. I didn't want to believe it at first—people protesting against *us* when we were putting our lives on the line for our country. The men in my outfit used to talk about it a lot. How could they do this to us? We swore they would pay, the hippies and draftcard burners. They would pay if we ever ran into them.

But the (prison-like VA) hospital had changed all that. It was the end of whatever belief I'd still had in what I'd done in Vietnam. Now I wanted to know what I had lost my legs for, why I and the others had gone at all. But it was still very hard for me to think of speaking out against the war, to think of joining those I'd once called traitors.

I was sitting alone in my apartment listening to the radio when I first heard the news about Kent State. Four students had just been shot in a demonstration against the invasion of Cambodia. For a moment there was a shock through my body. I felt like crying. The last time I had felt that way was the day Kennedy was killed.

The New Jersey Turnpike was packed with cars painted with flags and signs, and everywhere there were people hitching, holding up big cardboard peace symbols. You didn't have to ask where anyone was going. We were all going to the same place. Washington was a madhouse with buses and trucks and cars coming in from all directions.

We got a parking space and I gave up my tie and sweater for no shirt and a big red bandana around my head. Skip pushed the wheelchair for what seemed a mile or so. We could feel the tremendous tension. People were handing out leaflets reminding everyone that this was a nonviolent demonstration, and that no purpose would be served in violent confrontation. I remember feeling a little scared, the way I did before a firefight. After reading the leaflet I felt content that no one was going to get hurt.

Skip and I moved as close to the speakers' platform as we could and Skip lifted me out of my chair and laid me on my cushion. People were streaming into the Ellipse from all around us—an army of everyday people. There was a guy with a stereo/tape deck blasting out music, and dogs running after Frisbees on the lawn. The Hari Krishna people started to dance and the whole thing seemed like a weird carnival. But there was a warmth to it, a feeling that we were all together in a very important place. A young girl sat down next to me and handed me a canteen of cool water. "Here," she said, "have a drink." I drank it down and passed it to Skip who passed it to someone else. That was the feeling that day. We all seemed to be sharing everything.

We listened as the speakers one after another denounced the invasion of Cambodia and the slaying of the students at Kent State. The sun was getting very hot and Skip and I decided to move around. We wanted to get to the White House where Nixon was holed up, probably watching television. We were in a great sea of people, thousands and thousands all around us. We finally made it to Lafayette Park. On the other side of the avenue the government had lined up thirty or forty buses, making a huge wall between the people and the White House. I remember wondering back then why they had to put all those buses in front of the president. Was the government so afraid of its own people that it needed such a gigantic barricade?

127

I remember how the police came later that day, very suddenly, when we were watching the sun go down—a blue legion of police in cars and on motorcycles and others with angry faces on big horses. A tall cop walked into the crowd near the Reflecting Pool and read something into a bullhorn no one could make out. The drums stopped and a few of the naked people began to put their clothes back on. It was almost evening and with most of the invading army's forces heading back along the Jersey Turnpike, the blue legion had decided to attack. And they did— wading their horses into the pool, flailing their clubs, smashing skulls. People were running everywhere as gas cannisters began to pop. I couldn't understand why this was happening, why the police would attack the people, running them into the grass with their horses and beating them with their clubs. Two or three horses charged into the crowd at full gallop, driving the invading army into retreat toward the Lincoln Memorial. A girl was crying and screaming, trying to help her bleeding friend. She was yelling something about the pigs and kept stepping backward away from the horses and the flying clubs. For the first time that day I felt anger surge up inside me. I was no longer an observer, sitting in my car on the edge of a demonstration. I was right in the middle of it and it was ugly. Skip started pushing the chair as fast as he could up the path toward Lincoln Memorial. I kept turning, looking back. I wanted to shout back at the charging police, tell them I was a veteran.

I told Skip that I was never going to be the same. The demonstration had stirred something in my mind that would be there from now on. It was so different from boot camp and fighting in the war. There was a togetherness, just as there had been in Vietnam, but it was a togetherness of a different kind of people and for a much different reason. In the war we were killing and maiming people. In Washington on that Saturday afternoon in May we were trying to heal them and set them free.

Ron Kovic

from BORN ON THE FOURTH OF JULY

THE DAY THE AUDIENCE WALKED OUT ON ME, AND WHY

[*May 8th, 1970 Goucher College, Maryland*]

Like this it happened:
after the antiphonal reading from the psalms
and the dance of lamentation before the altar,
and the two poems, 'Life at War' and
'What Were They Like?'

I began my rap,
and said:
Yes, it is well that we have gathered
in this chapel to remember
the students shot at Kent State,

but let us be sure we know
our gathering is a mockery unless
we remember also
the black students shot at Orangeburg two years ago,
and Fred Hampton murdered in his bed
by the police only months ago.

And while I spoke the people
—girls, older women, a few men—
began to rise and turn
their backs to the altar and leave.

And I went on and said,
Yes, it is well that we remember
all of these, but let us be sure
we know it is hypocrisy
to think of them unless
we make our actions their memorial,
actions of militant resistance.

By then the pews were almost empty
and I returned to my seat and a man stood up
in the back of the quiet chapel
(near the wide-open doors through which
the green of May showed, and the long shadows
of late afternoon)
and said my words desecrated a holy place.

And a few days later
when some more students (black) were shot
at Jackson, Mississippi,
no one desecrated the white folks' chapel,
because no memorial service was held.

Denise Levertov

DARK WITH POWER

Dark with power, we remain
the invaders of our land, leaving
deserts where forests were,
scars where there were hills.

On the mountains, on the rivers
on the cities, on the farmlands
we lay weighted hands, our breath
potent with the death of all things.

Pray to us, farmers and villagers
of Viet Nam. Pray to us, mothers
and children of helpless countries.
Ask for nothing.

We are carried in the belly
of what we have become
toward the shambles of our triumph,
far from the quiet houses.

Fed with dying, we gaze
on our might's monuments of fire.
The world dangles from us
while we gaze.

Wendell Berry

ON BEING ASKED TO WRITE A POEM AGAINST THE WAR IN VIETNAM

Well I have and in fact
more than one and I'll
tell you this too

I wrote one against
Algeria that nightmare
and another against

Korea and another
against the one
I was in

and I don't remember
how many against
the three

when I was a boy
Abyssinia Spain and
Harlan County

and not one
breath was restored
to one

shattered throat
mans womans or childs
not one not

one
but death went on and on
never looking aside

except now and then like a child
with a furtive half-smile
to make sure I was noticing.

Hayden Carruth

THE BIRDS OF VIETNAM

O bright, O swift and bright,
you flashing among pandanus boughs
    (is that right? pandanus?)
under the great banyan, in and out
the dusky delicate bamboo groves
    (yes? banyan, bamboo?)
low, wide-winged, gliding
over the wetlands and drylands
    (but I have not seen you,
    I do not know your names,
    I do not know
    what I am talking about).

I have seen the road runner and the golden eagle,
the great white heron and the Kirtland's warbler,
    our own endangered species,
and I have worried about them. I have worried
about all our own, seen and unseen,
whooping cranes, condors, white-tailed kites,
and the ivory-bills (certainly gone, all gone!)
the ones we have harried, murdered, driven away
as if we were the Appointed Avengers,
    the Destroyers, the Wrathful Ones
out of our ancestors' offended hearts
at the cruel beginning of the world.
But for what? for whom? why?
    Nobody knows.

And why, in my image of that cindered country,
should I waste my mourning? I will never have

132

enough. Think of the children there,
insane little crusted kids at the beckoning fire,
think of the older ones, burned, crazy with fear,
sensible beings who can know hell, think
of their minds exploding, their hearts flaming.

I do think. But today,
O mindless, O heartless, in and out
the dusky delicate groves,
your hell becomes mine, simply
and without thought, you maimed, you
poisoned in your nests, starved
in the withered forests.
   O mindless, heartless,
   you never invented hell.
We say flesh turns to dust, though more often
a man-corpse too, yet your feathers
   retain life's color
long afterward, even in the robes
   of barbarous kings,
still golden the trogon feather,
still bright the egret plume, and the crest
of the bower bird will endure forever
almost. You will always remind us of what
   the earth has been.

O bright, swift, gleaming
in dusky groves,
I mourn you.
O mindless, heartless, I can't
help it, I have so loved
   this world.

Hayden Carruth

Peace the great meaning has not been defined.
When we say peace as a word, war
As a flare of fire leaps across our eyes.
We went to this school. Think war;
Cancel war, we were taught.
What is left is peace.
No, peace is not left, it is no canceling;
The fierce and human peace is our deep power
Born to us of wish and responsibility.

Muriel Rukeyser

THE HOSTAGES

When I stand with these three
My new brothers my new sister
These who bind themselves offering
Hostages to go at a word, hostages
to go deeper here among our own cities
When I look into your faces
Karl, Martin, Andrea.

When I look into your faces
Offered men and women, I can speak,
And I speak openly on the church steps,
At the peace center saying: We affirm
Our closeness forever with the eyes in Asia,
Those who resist the forces we resist.
One more hostage comes forward, his eyes: Joe,
With Karl, Martin, Andrea, me.

And now alone in the river-watching room,
Allen, your voice comes, the deep prophetic word.
And we are one more, Joe, Andrea, Karl, Martin,
Allen, me.   The hostages.   Reaching.   Beginning.

Muriel Rukeyser

BRINGING

Bringing their life   these young
bringing their life   rise from their wakings
bringing their life   come to a place
where they make their gifts

The grapes of life of death   of transformation
round they hang at hand   desires   like peace
or seed of revolutions that make all things new
and must be lived out, washed in rivers, and themselves made new
and bringing their life   the young   they reach
in their griefs   their mistakes   their discovering
bringing their life   they touch   they take
bringing their life   they come to a place

It is raining fire   they are bringing their life
their sex speaks for them   their ideas all speak
their acts arrive   bringing their life entire
They resist a system of wars and rewards
They offer their open faces   they offer their bodies
They offer their hands   bringing their life entire
They offer their life   they are their own gifts
Make life   resist   resist   make life
Bringing their life entire   they come to this moment
Bringing their life entire   they come to this place

Muriel Rukeyser

COMING HOME

When I first got home I didn't want to hear anything about Viet Nam. I wanted to get it out of my mind. All the newspapers that I got over in Viet Nam—it always seemed that somebody was doing something about the war, trying to end it: the Paris Peace talks, the Peace Movement, you know, different groups back in the States, different Congressmen—everybody was trying to do something to end it, and everything that was being done seemed to be published in the newspapers. But then, one day I picked up the paper to see what was being done this week. And there wasn't anything there; not on the front page, not anywhere. Here I'd been trying to survive every day, really scared, and so glad that I was back. I knew a lot of my friends were still over there, and the people back here weren't interested in the War.

I mean, you just look back after you come back from Viet Nam, and you can look at things a little more objectively. You take a look at things a little more objectively. You take a look at the attitude that the Americans had toward the Vietnamese people. We just treated them as menial servants, sometimes like they were animals or something. During my last two months over there, I took care of the Vietnamese when they came in to clean up. We would watch them when they did jobs like doing some carpentry work on one of the barracks or digging some holes or changing some tires or cleaning the hooches. And I remember I used to work with them. I had the job of watching over them so that they did the work, but I used to help them. And some lifer would come by and tell me not to work with them, just to watch them and make sure they did it. I thought that was pretty bad. I wanted to work with them: why couldn't I? The whole attitude was that they were low class subservient people—it was a racist thing. We would treat them as a subservient race.

We weren't a liberation army; we were an occupation army, and that can be clearly seen when you're there. After you're over there awhile, you see the whole Vietnamese land being destroyed. They don't have enough to eat because we've defoliated their land. I've seen planes go over valleys when I was there, spraying the land with defoliants, and when I've gone through villages I've seen children really looking thin—you can see their ribs—and you wonder why they don't have enough to eat. You see all this rice growing around, but it isn't enough to feed the Vietnamese. I found out later that somewhere around half the rice consumed in Viet Nam comes from Texas, when at one time South Vietnam was one of the world's largest rice producers. At one base camp where I was, we used to feed them the garbage after a few days of collecting garbage. It was at this fire base south of Duc Pho. We would collect the garbage and then we would drive it down to the nearby village and dump it right outside the village, and all the people would be there, ready, waiting for the garbage, and they would just walk through the garbage and start eating whatever was there. They would collect some of it and put it in containers and take it back to the village for the rest of their families, I suppose. And that made me sick to see that happening, because they just didn't have enough food there. Before we were there, they did. And now that we were there, supposedly helping them, they didn't.

Then I came back home to find out that millions of Americans go to bed hungry. I think a Kennedy Commission came out with that. In the U.S. we are spending 65 to 70 cents out of every dollar on the war for defense and yet we can't even feed the people here at home. We can't even provide a means of living for them.

A lot of veterans come home unemployed, they can't even find a means of living, yet we're spending millions and millions of dollars destroying a country when we could be spending this same money developing our own and finding means of living for people here.

I looked around for a job for a month after I came back, but I couldn't find any because of the inflation. And here I had gone over and fought so that I could live in this country, and I couldn't even get a job. You know they say, "Well, you aren't trained in anything.". . . the only thing I had been trained in was to kill. I had been trained in the infantry, and there wasn't a market for that over here. So I couldn't get a job. Before I went over, they said, "You're 1-A and you'll probably get drafted, so you can't get a job." So I got rid of that. I went over and got rid of the 1-A and came back and did the military duty and then I came back, and they still wouldn't hire me.

You're told to fight for your country and serve it, and you come back here and all these are wrong: the unemployment, the hunger, the pollution. You can't even come back to clean air. You can't even breathe clean air any more. And yet all this money is being spent on destruction and yet you come back to a situation where you're constantly struggling to live and to have a means of living and to survive through the pollution and the unemployment. I mean, where are our priorities? To destroy one country thousands of miles away, to destroy the people over there and not to provide the things that we need that are so vital for living in this country.

So I'm really agains the Viet Nam war and our total involvement there, because while we're destroying an entire country over there, we're not doing anything over here. I think we should pull out of Viet Nam immediately and allow all the Vietnamese to solve their own problems in their own land, and for us to come back here and solve our problems here.

John Beitzel

VETERAN'S DAY

Never mind the day;
Cricket lost his legs
in the war. At night
he has nightmares
and rubs his crutches
against his watch,
which has only one hand.

Look at the moon!
See how the dead
shed light and draw
sequins on the water
that keep Cricket awake nights.

Richard Levine

THE SPOILS OF WAR

When it rains
he can feel
the shrapnel still in him
like anger and fear;

he can feel its prick
embedded deep,
rusting
his vision of peace.

Richard Levine

NIGHTS IN SHINING ARMOR

I have this suit
of armor,
and I can't get it off.

Though it is invisible
it squeaks, and I know
I will die in it;

so when people hear it and ask,
"Are you responsible
for that?"

I want to lower my visor.
Like all suits of armor
mine is haunted.

It has taken years to feel
through this metal,
and sleep in this suit.

Richard Levine

ME

the seed bringer
the meat finder
the plant grower
the tool-maker
creator/preserver/destroyer
the wanderer warrior &
African scientist me
sailor-poet & father-explorer
the priest-king me
still needs a woman
still loves children
still kills his brother/self
still must find his way
to be human-me/man

Horace Coleman

THE SOLDIER

Crawling through the battlefield,
he shoots! Splatter of blood and brain.
He sees other faces in the bushes,
eyes their eyes and aims his gun.

The war is over. Still he holds his gun.
Within   him is a battlefield.
They have mined his brain.
It's a trap of treacherous bushes.

Where there's a bird, he sees a gun.
Where there's a lake, a battlefield.
The battlefield is locked inside his brain.
He hides in bushes and aims his gun.

Rachelle Benveniste

A U.S. INFANTRY COMPANY JUST CAME THROUGH HERE!

IF YOU HAD BEEN VIETNAMESE---

We might have burned your house

We might have shot your dog

We might have shot you...

We might have raped your wife and daughter

We might have turned you over to your government for torture

We might have taken souvenirs from your property

We might have shot things up a bit...

We might have done ALL these things to you

    and your whole TOWN!

If it doesn't bother you that American soldiers
do these things every day to the Vietnamese
simply because they are "Gooks", then picture YOURSELF
as one of the silent VICTIMS.

HELP US TO END THE WAR BEFORE THEY TURN YOUR SON INTO A BUTCHER
    or a corpse.

VIETNAM VETERANS AGAINST THE WAR
156 Fifth Avenue, New York City, New York 10010

Sheldon Ramsdell

VETERANS' MARCH TO VALLEY FORGE

From Jockey Hollow in the hills above Morristown,
down through Bernardsville, White House Station,
Flemington on the Jersey side, across Bucks County
on the Pennsylvania bank, to Valley Forge
a hundred veterans of the latest war
stalk the roadsides of the Delaware River backcountry,
streaming into sleepy small towns in combat gear
and grabbing suspect civilians
from storefronts and sidewalks and village greens,
holding interrogation sessions on courthouse steps
and firefights in shopping center parking lots,
startling passersby uninitiated to the taste
of outdoor guerrilla theater
performed by grim young men wearing war medals
and wound scars to prove their expertise.

It is Labor Day weekend, end of summer 1970.
The Sixties are dead and buried
with the bodies of those college students who got shot
dead for too much protest, so who are these wise guys?
the stares from the colder local drivers
on the backroads seem to say.
Some travelers and homebodies do a double take,
honk the horn, flash fingers in a ''V'' for peace.
Some knots of hate turn out along roadsides
to heckle, wave the flag, scream out
''Go back to Russia where you came from!''
One young man aims a shotgun from his front porch.
''Go to Vietnam!''
some armchair patriots shout at men who've been.

Three days, eighty miles the peace marchers press
through the heat and the hecklers, the state
police and FBI surveillance net,
trailing camera crews, tramping the old roads
Washington's winter soldiers took between campaigns,
seeking the source of America's faltering promise,
seeking the help of their countrymen.

Jan Barry

"COMPANYYY!"

"PRESENT—

ARMS!"

"BREAK—ARMS!"

Vietnam Veterans Against the War, Valley Forge,
Pennsylvania, September 7, 1970

Vietnam Veterans Against the War requests your presence at the Winter Soldier Investigation (an inquiry into U.S. War Crimes in Indochina).

The hearings will be held at the Howard Johnson's New Center Motor Lodge, Detroit, Michigan, January 31, February 1 and 2, 1971. The purpose of this investigation is to preclude the further scapegoating of individual soldiers for what is in fact Official United States Military Policy.

R.S.V.P.

WINTER SOLDIER INVESTIGATION

"Over the border they send us to kill and to fight for a cause they've long ago forgotten." These lines of Paul Simon's recall to Vietnam veterans the causes for which we went to fight in Vietnam and the outrages we were part of because the men who sent us had long ago forgotten the meaning of the words.

We went to preserve the peace and our testimony will show that we have set all of Indochina aflame. We went to defend the Vietnamese people and the testimony will show that we are committing genocide against them. We went to fight for freedom and our testimony will show that we have turned Vietnam into a series of concentration camps. We went to guarantee the right of self-determination to the people of South Vietnam and our testimony will show that we are forcing a corrupt and dictatorial government upon them. We went to work toward the brotherhood of man and our testimony will show that our strategy and tactics are permeated with racism. We went to protect America and our testimony will show why our country is being torn apart by what we are doing in Vietnam.

In the bleak winter of 1776 when the men who had enlisted in the summer were going home because the war was hard and their enlistments were over, Tom Paine wrote, ''these are the times that try men's souls. The summer soldier and the sunshine patriot will in this crisis shrink from the service of his country, but he that stands it now deserves the love and thanks of man and woman.'' Like the winter soldiers of 1776 who stayed after they had served their time, we veterans of Vietnam know that America is in grave danger. What threatens our country is not Redcoats or even Reds; it is our crimes that are destroying our national security unity by separating those of our countrymen who deplore these acts from those of our countrymen who refuse to examine what is being done in America's name.

The Winter Soldier Investigation is not a mock trial. There will be no phony indictments; there will be no verdict against Uncle Sam. In these three days, over a hundred Vietnam veterans will present straightforward testimony—direct testimony—about acts which are war crimes under international law. Acts which these men have seen and participated in. Acts which are the inexorable result of national policy. The vets will testify in panels arranged by the combat units in which they fought so that it will be easy to see the policy of each division and thus the larger policy.

We are here to bear witness not against America, but against those policy makers who are perverting America. We echo Mark Twain's indictment of the war crimes committed during the Phillipine insurrection: ''We have invited our clean young men to soldier a discredited musket and do bandit's work under a flag which bandits have been accustomed to fear not to follow. We cannot conceal from ourselves that privately we are a little troubled about our uniform. It is one of our prides; it is acquainted with honor; it is familiar with great deeds and noble. We love it; we revere it. And so this errand it is on makes us uneasy. And our flag, another pride of ours, the chiefest. We have worshipped it so and when we have seen it in far lands, glimpsing it unexpectedly in that strange sky, waving its welcome and benediction to us, we have caught our breaths and uncovered our heads for a moment for the thought of what it was to us and the great ideals it stood for. Indeed, we must do something about these things. It is easily managed. We can have just our usual flag with the white stripes painted black and the stars replaced by the skull and cross-bones.''

We are ready to let the testimony say it all.

William Crandell
[*former 1/Lt., Americal Div. in Vietnam, 1969*]

AMERICA

Now,
Before the napalm-scorched earth
consumes the blood
of
would-be-fathers
and
have-been-sons
of
daughters spread-eagled
and
mothers on the run.
Reflect.
See what you've become,

Amerika.

Al Hubbard

THE AMERICAN WAR

I'm a Seminola Indian. If you took the Vietnamese war, or the American war, as it is, and compared it to the Indian wars a hundred years ago, it would be the same thing. All the massacres were the same. Nowadays they use chemical warfare; back then they put smallpox in the blankets and gave them to the Indians. You could just go right on down the line and name them out and they would be the same thing.

One thing about racism, is that I have grown up with it all my life. When I was small I was exposed to it. When I watched TV or something and watched the Indians and the cavalry, I would cheer for the cavalry. That's how bad it was.

Right now a lot of Indian people are thinking about the old ways. Way back, they had something good. And then people started getting into a money bag, and that's when it all happened. When we made treaties long ago, it was for as long as the grass shall grow and as long as the rivers shall flow. The way things are going now, one of these days the grass isn't going to grow. . . and the rivers aren't going to flow. . . .

Evan Haney

HEY! REMEMBER ME?

I was that tiny premature baby
born just before Christmas, 1942, at St. Mary's
    Hospital--
Remember how you all said I'd never make it?
Then there was the time I read from the Bible
when the preacher got sick just before his sermon.
Remember how you all said
''Hey, you ought to consider the ministry!''
How about the last second basket I made
that beat Perryville and took us to the state
    tournament--
Remember how you all cheered and said I'd make
    the pros?
And when I was chosen Best Actor and won
the college public speaking contest both the same
    year--
Remember how proud you were?
You slapped my back and shook my hand.
Then came Basic Training, Advanced Infantry Training
and Infantry Officer Candidate School--
Remember how impressed you all were that
    I became an officer?
Then came Vietnam, where I did my job,
got a Bronze Star and Purple Heart--
Remember how proud you were when I came home?

But now when I ask why I had to destroy those gentle
    people,
when I question the policies and decisions
that made me into a killer--
When I ask you why you never asked why,
you treat me like a stranger.
Hey! Remember me?

Larry Rottmann

WE DID A TERRIBLE THING

In Vietnam we have a situation where never has there been such a disparity of power since the days when Mussolini and Count Ciano went into Abyssinia to slaughter the spear-carrying troops of Haile Selassie. We have brought wondrous tons of ordinance, hundreds of thousands of men, Dr. Strangelove weaponry. We have used an air force against a country that has none. We have used a navy against a country that has none. . . .

We build forts in Vietnam to protect villages, or so we told the Vietnamese. And at the first shot fired at Tet in 1968 we destroyed the villages to protect the fort. District Eight in Saigon was leveled brick by brick, to the ground, to secure an area where North Vietnamese Catholics had come to the South (after the Communist-led rebellion defeated the French colonial army) in 1954. We leveled that area to protect a bridge.

Our country has set out very systematically to kill whatever number of people are necessary in Vietnam to stop them from resisting whatever it is we are trying to impose on that country. This, I think is policy. I think we have established that policy here at these hearings.

For those of you who have never been in service and have listened to this testimony, you might well be amazed at how our people—our men, our boys, our sons—could do some of these things that they described in this room. Otherwise normal individuals, creating terror, torture, wanton destruction. How could they have done this? How could they have been changed that dramatically in eight short weeks of basic training? I think the fact that so much can be done to so many men by so few people is the greatest testament to the fact that our colleges, our high schools, our everyday life is nothing but pre-basic training.

The men did not become racists when they entered the service. They grew up with it. It was taught to them and it was taught to them in our schools. The idea that the United States has a God-given right to go into any country and take out its raw materials at an advantage to ourselves is not something that they learned in Vietnam. They learned it in our schools. They learned it from their mothers, fathers, their sisters and their brothers, their uncles. They learned it from all of us.

We did a terrible thing to a lot of men in Vietnam and we're still doing it. I don't know who the ultimate victims in Vietnam will be. Will it be those who went from the U.S. to fight in it, or the Vietnamese who tried to resist? I do know this, having met and talked with many Vietnamese who have gone through worse hardships than anyone in this room, that they, at least, do not seem to have lost their humanity in the process. But I fear that many of us, if we don't shorten up and get the message out, we will have lost our humanity beyond redemption.

I remember in 1966, I testified to many of the things that have been testified to here. I was very lonely. Thank God, I'm not lonely anymore. But still it's a terrible way to gain company—to have men do these things. We have to get it out...

There are many things that you, as veterans, with this experience can do. You must not forget that, in fact, there are still 3,000,000 men in uniform—a hell of a lot of them still in Vietnam and a hell of a lot of them to end up in Vietnam, Laos and Cambodia. Start working with them. Start working with those who have not yet been drafted, and talk to them, and make the reality of the war known to them. And talk to your families. Over 40 percent of all the adult males in this country are veterans. That's something we have to turn around. We have to stop producing veterans.

For those of you who are veterans and are working and have been working for some time, keep working. And some day you will be ex-veterans, and we'll be just people again.

Don Duncan
[*former Master Sergeant, 5th Special Forces in Vietnam '64-'65*]

Inside the photograph:

Pick a Winner From The Star's Racing Page

CAPITAL SPECIAL

The Evening Star

Veterans Staying In Camp on Mall

Jim Pathe

RETURNING WAR MEDALS TO CONGRESS

WASHINGTON, D.C. April 23, 1971

"We now strip ourselves of these medals of courage and heroism. . . these citations for gallantry and exemplary service. . . We cast these away as symbols of shame, dishonor and inhumanity," announced a tall, bearded Marine veteran, Jack Smith, before flinging his war medals onto the steps of the U.S. Capitol.

"Our tale is one of a Vietnamese people whose hearts were broken, not won" by an American military command "not concerned with lives, but with body counts," said Smith as he stood at the head of a long, single-file line of several hundred Vietnam veterans waiting to discard what soon became a trash heap of Silver and Bronze Stars, Purple Hearts, Air Medals, combat badges, campaign ribbons.

Despite a week of intense lobbying and nationally-televised peace demonstrations in and outside government offices, the former Marine staff sergeant reported that in the halls of Congress, for the most part, the war veterans had met "closed doors and closed minds."

One after another, the jungle uniform-clad veterans hurled their medals over a temporary crowd control fence across the Capitol front, some hobbling quickly away, some weeping, some silent and grim as death, some shouting to the assembled news reporters, supporters and crowds of curiosity seekers: "Here's my merit badges for murder. . . My parents told me that if I really did come down here and turned in my medals, that they never wanted anything more to do with me. . . I'm not proud of these medals, I'm not proud of what I did to receive them. . . Listen! you newsmen, we're not giving you the medals. We're turning them in to the country—don't touch them!. . . I'm here because I was in Vietnam. I know what I did and it was wrong. . . I'm prouder today of the service I have given my country than at any time I was over there. . . I'd like to say just one thing for the people of Vietnam. I'm sorry. I hope that someday I can return to Vietnam and help rebuild that country we tore apart.''

Jim Pathe

Jim Pathe

TESTIMONY TO CONGRESS

In 1970 at West Point Vice President Agnew said ''some glamorize the criminal misfits of society while our best men die in Asian rice paddies to preserve the freedom which most of those misfits abuse,'' and this was used as a rallying point for our effort in Vietnam.

But for us, as boys in Asia whom the country was supposed to support, his statement is a terrible distortion from which we can only draw a very deep sense of revulsion, and hence the anger of some of the men who are here in Washington today. It is a distortion because we in no way consider ourselves the best men of this country, because those he calls misfits were standing up for us in a way that nobody else in this country dared to, because so many who have died would have returned as quadriplegics and amputees, and they lie forgotten in Veterans Administration Hospitals in this country which fly the flag which so many have chosen as their own personal symbol, and we cannot consider ourselves America's best men when we are ashamed of and hated what we were called on to do in Southeast Asia.

In our opinion, and from our experiences, there is nothing in South Vietnam, nothing which could happen that realistically threatens the United States of America. And to attempt to justify the loss of one American life in Vietnam, Cambodia or Laos, by linking such loss to the preservation of freedom, which those misfits supposedly abuse, is to us the height of criminal hypocrisy, and it is that kind of hypocrisy which we feel has torn this country apart.

We found that not only was it a civil war, an effort by a people who had for years been seeking their liberation from any colonial influence whatsoever, but also found that the Vietnamese whom we had enthusiastically molded after our own image were hard put to take up the fight against the threat we were supposedly saving them from.

We found most people didn't even know the difference between communism and democracy. They only wanted to work in rice paddies without helicopters straffing them and bombs with napalm burning their villages and tearing their country apart. They wanted everything to do with the war, particularly with this foreign presence of the United States of America, to leave them alone in peace, and they practised the art of survival by siding with whichever military force was present at a particular time, be it Viet Cong, North Vietnamese or American.

We found that all too often American men were dying in those rice paddies for want of support from their allies. We saw first-hand how monies from American taxes was used for a corrupt dictatorial regime. We saw that many people in this country had a one-sided idea of who was kept free by our flag, as blacks provided the highest percentage of casualties. We saw Vietnam ravaged equally by American bombs as well as by search and destroy missions, as well as by Viet Cong terrorism, and yet we listened while this country tried to blame all of the havoc on the Viet Cong.

We rationalized destroying villages in order to save them. We saw America lose her sense of morality as she accepted very cooly a My Lai and refused to give up the image of American soldiers who hand out chocolate bars and chewing gum.

We learned the meaning of free fire zones, shooting anything that moves, and we watched while America placed a cheapness on the lives of orientals.

We watched the United States falsification of body counts, in fact, the glorification of body counts. We listened while month after month we were told the back of the enemy was about to break. We fought using weapons against "oriental human beings", we fought using weapons against those people which I do not believe this country would dream of using were we fighting in the European theater or let us say a non-third world people theater, and so we watched while men charged up hills because a general said that that hill had to be taken, and after losing one platoon or two platoons they marched away to leave the hill for re-occupation by the North Vietnamese because we watched pride allow the most unimportant of battles to be blown into extravaganzas, because we couldn't lose, and we couldn't retreat, and because it didn't matter how many American bodies were lost to prove that point, and so there were Hamburger Hills and Khe Sanhs and Hill 881s and Fire Base 6s and so many others.

Now we are told that the men who fought there must watch quietly while American lives are lost so that we can exercise the incredible arrogance of Vietnamizing the Vietnamese.

Each day to facilitate the process by which the United States washes her hands of Vietnam, someone has to give up his life so that the United States doesn't have to admit something that the entire world already knows, so that we can't say that we have made a mistake. Someone has to die so the President Nixon won't be, and these are his words, "the first President to lose a war."

We are asking Americans to think about that because how do you ask a man to be the last man to die in Vietnam? How do you ask a man to be the last man to die for a mistake? But we are trying to do that, and we are doing it with thousands of rationalizations, and if you read carefully the President's last speech to the people of this country, you can see that he says, and says clearly, "but the issue, gentlemen, the issue is communism, and the question is whether or not we will leave that country to the communists or whether or not we will try to give it hope to be a free people." But the point is they are not a free people now under us, they are not a free people, and we cannot fight communism all over the world, and I think we should have learned that lesson by now.

But the problem of veterans goes beyond this personal problem, because you think about a poster in this country with a picture of Uncle Sam and the picture says, "I want you." And a young man comes out of high school and says, "that is fine, I am going to serve my country," and he goes to Vietnam and he shoots and he kills and he does his job or maybe he doesn't kill, maybe he just goes and he comes back, and when he gets back to this country he finds that he isn't really wanted because the largest unemployment figure in the country, the largest corps of unemployed in this country are veterans of this war, and of those veterans, 33% of the unemployed are black. That means one out of every ten of the nation's unemployed is a veteran of Vietnam.

We are asking here in Washington for some action, action from the Congress of the United States of America which has the power to raise and maintain armies, and which by the Constitution also has the power to declare war.

We have come here, not to the President, because we believe that this body can be responsive to the will of the people, and we believe that the will of the people says that we should be out of Vietnam now.

We are also here to ask, and we are here to ask vehemently, where are the leaders of our country, where is the leadership? We are here to ask where McNamara, Rostow, Bundy, Gilpatric and so many others, where are they now that we, the men whom they sent off to war, have returned? These are commanders who have deserted their troops, and there is no more serious crime in the law of war. The Army says they never leave their wounded. The Marines say they never leave even their dead. These men have left all the casualties and retreated behind a pious shield of public rectitude. They have left the real stuff of their reputations bleaching behind them in the sun in this country.

Finally, this administration has done us the ultimate dishonor. They have attempted to disown us and the sacrifices we made for this country. In their blindness and fear they have tried to deny that we are veterans or that we served in Nam. We do not need their testimony. Our own scars and stumps of limbs are witness enough for others and for ourselves.

We wish that a merciful God could wipe away our own memories of that service as easily as this administration has wiped their memories of us. But all that they have done and all that they can do by this denial is to make more clear than ever our own determination to undertake one last mission, to search out and destroy the last vestige of this barbaric war, to pacify our own hearts, to conquer the hate and the fear that have driven this country these last ten years and more. And so when in thirty years from now when our brothers go down the street without a leg, without an arm, or a face, and small boys ask why, we will be able to say "Vietnam" and not mean a desert, not a filthy obscene memory, but mean instead the place where America finally turned and where soldiers like us helped in the turning.

John Kerry

Jim Pathe

WE'RE LEAVING INDOCHINA

We're leaving Indochina tons of steel with fire,
    death, agony and chaos every day.

I see Nixon on a wheel like my mouse had—
    mouthing his manifestos.
He thinks we're watching him
While the generals keep up their bloody play—
Well, maybe he is right in that.
He says, ''I am going to China,''
As if that is to bear the world up—

While the world of untold other human beings
Collapses day after day, hour after hour,
Under the bombs we are leaving Indochina.

Joan Nicholson

July 20, 1971

CAMBODIAN TEMPLE RUBBING

three male warriors
stand with right legs
poised in the air.

in their left hand
they hold bows
with no bow strings.

they wear pointed hats
and crocodile tails
to frighten the game.

each warrior faces west, smiling.
there are no clouds
behind them. no sky.

these rubbings are rare.

years after the bombings
there are no temples.

Franz Douskey

158

THE DEMARKATION LINE

The unknown terrifies;
I no longer stand in awe of Hell,
for once I passed that line
where his brown eyes dulled forever,
I found defoliated trees,
impaled skulls, dried ears
in surreal dreams variegated
with the sickening pinks of napalm
while flotsam cymbals crashed.
I saw Satan tremble to hear
the dreaded curse, ''Nam.''
I cannot talk about it rationally,
and I saw only
the woman side of Hell—
but the myths were right:
it is eternal.

Margaret Key Biggs

THE LANGUAGE OF TORTURERS

When I came back from Vietnam in 1967 I did not yet have a sense that our involvement was outrageous or criminal, but I strongly believed that it must be ended. I began to look for allies among other officials who had left Vietnam or left office disillusioned with the war. And I came up against a phenomenon that has challenged me ever since, both to understand and to deal with: the apparent lack of any strong sense of personal responsibility on the part of many of these individuals to take effective steps to help end the war. Despite their own involvement, and despite their disaffection, most of them seemed unwilling to take any more active part in antiwar efforts than they had while they were still serving the Government.

But neither had my year in the Pentagon taught me to read the "contingency plans" and proposals that had passed through my own hands with the same eyes that my wife and children brought to them six years later. Here is some of the language they read in the Pentagon papers about our bombing policy:

"We all accept the will of the DRV (Democratic Republic of Vietnam) as the real target";

"Judging by experience during the last war, the resumption of bombing after a pause would be even more painful to the population of North Vietnam than a fairly steady rate of bombing";

". . . 'water-drip' technique. . .";

"It is important not to 'kill the hostage' by destroying the North Vietnamese assets inside the 'Hanoi donut'";

"Fast/full squeeze. . ." option versus "Progressive squeeze-and-talk";

". . . the 'hot-cold' treatment. . . the objective of 'persuading' Hanoi, which would dictate a program of painful surgical strikes separated by fairly long gaps. . .";

". . . our 'salami-slice' bombing program. . .";

". . . ratchet. . .";

". . . one more turn of the screw. . ."

These were phrases — written by senior officials I worked with and respected — that I had read and discussed in offices in the Pentagon and State, often in disapproval of their contents yet without ever seeing or hearing them as my wife did when she characterized them, in horror, as "the language of torturers."

Among the dozen or so former officials who (initially) possessed copies of the Pentagon Papers, and were thus physically in a position to draw public conclusions based on them or even to reveal them to Congress and the people, there were at least two differences in myself that sharpened my sense of personal responsibility. Only two of us — I became the second that September (1969), and a year later there were still only three — had actually read the whole of the McNamara Study, or even any substantial part of it; only the two, then three, of us knew the story the Pentagon Papers told and had been changed by it. And of the whole dozen — the rest of whom had served at higher levels than these three — only one, myself, had ever lived in Vietnam, or had Vietnamese friends, had worked in the countryside and seen the war close at hand. In the words of a poster I saw recently, "There came a time when the people of Vietnam were as real to me as my own hands."

The months in Vietnam between 1965 and 1967 had changed me in ways that the previous year of reading high-level cables in Washington could not; and many of those memories changed character abruptly when the Pentagon Papers stripped away all legitimate rationales for what we were doing.

Within a few weeks or months from September (1969) the President would probably be committing himself publicly to the course of indefinite involvement I had heard privately described. Only Congress and the public—newly informed by "authoritative" warnings and, perhaps, by documentary evidence on the illegitimate origins and hopeless prospects of the war—might act to dissuade or prevent the President from pursuing the American war in Vietnam carried on by his four predecessors.

To ask myself, a man who had spent the last decade serving four of those five Presidents, to act on such perceptions was asking me to jump out of my skin. Something harder than risking it: that I had done already, along with some three million, mostly younger Americans who had gone to Vietnam. Most of us had seen our going as the response of loyal Americans to our President; until recently, few had supposed that might conflict with serving the legitimate interests of our country. What was needed now, to go beyond that reflex response, was the inspiration to find in oneself loyalties long unconsulted, deeper and broader than loyalty to the President: loyalties to America's founding concepts, to our Constitutional system, to countrymen, to one's own humanity—and to our "allies," the people we were bombing.

At this point it was other young Americans who helped me by their example. That same month of August, 1969, that I began to read the origins of the war and to learn the President's plans, I met for the first time, face-to-face, Americans who were on their way to prison for refusing to collaborate in an unjust war. I found them to be sober, intelligent, principled; they showed, in fact, the dedication I had respected in many officials I had known in Vietnam, but they were acting on different premises, which I now shared. These personal acts of "witness" gave me what reading alone could not.

In October, I joined my five colleagues at Rand in the first critical statement on Vietnam policy addressed to the public that any of us had ever signed: a letter to the New York Times calling for U.S. unilateral withdrawal within one year. At the same time, without the knowledge of anyone at Rand, I acted privately to reveal the information in the Pentagon Papers beginning with the Senate Foreign Relations Committee.

As it worked out, nearly twenty months went by before the information finally reached the public and the rest of Congress (or, for that matter, the Executive, which till then had neglected totally to unlock and study its own copies of the McNamara Study). . .

In releasing the Pentagon Papers I acted in hope I still hold: that truths that changed me could help Americans free themselves and other victims from our longest war.

Daniel Ellsberg

FIFTEENTH DAY OF THE FOURTH MONTH OF THE YEAR 1972

We called it
Resistance Day
and a bunch of us
gathered downtown
at the state capitol building
to make public
our acts of resistance to the war.
It was a small group
maybe twenty or twenty-five.
One by one members of the group
rose up from the grass
and walked to the microphone
and, speaking through the mike to the crowd,
told
      their name
      and their method of resistance
      and a little bit about why.

When they told their names
they were the names of real people,
      friends,
      citizens,
      neighbors,
      close friends,
      good folks.

When they told of their resistance
they spoke of
    refusing to pay income taxes to buy death
      and refusing to pay the phone tax which was levied to buy war
      and refusing to collaborate with the draft.

When they told of why
they spoke of
    their god
    their conscience
    the friends they left in Vietnam
      when they were there to kill
      both American and Vietnamese friends
      the planes and troops on alert here at home in our own state
      the faceless bureaucracy that demands their money or their life
      a two-year-old son
      our heritage of life, liberty and pursuit of happiness
      courts that do not allow arguments about morality or conscience
And then one of my friends
(who as a child had barely escaped the Gestapo)
pointed out to us
the flowering dogwood trees
      around us like white puffs of smoke
and the red azaleas
      like cool fire licking at the building
and then my friend spoke of
she spoke
of white phosphorus
      which burns for a week in the flesh of a child
and of
      falling fire from the sky which consumes villages.

Tonight on the TV it was announced that they have bombed Haiphong.
No matter what we do, it is not yet enough.

L. Russell Herman, Jr.

GLIDING BASKETS

"Eight Six Foxtrot — Eight Six Foxtrot.
This is One One Zulu. Over."

    The woman in blue
    Carried the weight swiftly, with grace,
    Her face hidden by her
    Conical rice straw hat.

"One One Zulu — this is Eight Six Foxtrot. Go."
"Roger Eight Six. I have Fire Mission.
Dink in the open, Grid: Bravo Sierra,
Five Six Niner, Four Six Five, Range:
Three thousand, Proximity: Eight hundred. Over."

    The two heavy baskets
    Balanced on tips
    Of the springing Chogi stick
    Glided close to the hard smooth path.

"Read back, One One Zulu."
"Roger Copy, Eight Six."
"Shot, on the way, wait."
"Shot out, Eight Six."

    A sighing 105mm round slides through its parabola
    Then the explosive tearing at the steel which surrounds it,
    And the shrapnel catches the gliding baskets,
    And they crumple with the woman in blue.

Frank A. Cross, Jr.

near An Trang
August 14, 1969

B-52'S AT HOME

Black ones
—For night missions
Over NVN?
Camouflaged ones
—For sitting
At Utapao?
Silver ones
—For H-bombs
To keep us free?

They all fly
Over my farm,
With necks outstretched,
Tails pouring with dysentery:
Rolls of black smoke—
Racing for cocktail hour
At the officer's club on Castle.
Bomb doors locked and shut,
Their wheels are down
Like ready talons.

My fields are smooth,
My ditches run straight,
My house still stands,
—But under the terrible
Swept-back, swift shadows:
                          I shudder.

Frank A. Cross, Jr.

Chowchilla, Cal.
June 5, 1972

AT THE RED RIVER

for Madame Nguyen Thi Binh & Jane Fonda

Over rippling waists of ricefields
and smouldering hearths,
a sudden storm of moon craters
caves in the thatched huts
They scorch open the villager's body.
Skies abscess fat with ash,
and the shit of the Pentagon's high priests,
smart bombs, TV bombs, Nixon bombs,
pummel the gates of the dikes.

To consent to genocide
profanes that embrace
making us a people.
Deathmongers gorge on silent consent.
They sculpt their imperial flag with it,
twitch with pleasure
behind desks
hearing the maimed cry.

Two tears kneel down in your heart
like prayers
ascending in the people's abundant wellsprings
of faith and enduring will.
Your undulating lament
familiar to roots and children,
camouflage and the cold,
blood and the burials,
sails a single wind across
the blue pampas of the Pacific,
dark, iridescent shoals,
the palms, the reefs,
abandoned coral,
to the rooftops and streets
of the world.

Now, beside ancestral torches
flickering in the underground
where all tributaries begin
their gaunt and crystalline journeys,
a lily climbs up through the earth,
and your sorrow become for us
all we ever wanted of the rain.

Doug Yamamoto

BLACK HOLE
(*George Knowlton*)

IN THAI BINH (PEACE) PROVINCE

for Muriel and Jane

I've used up all my film on bombed hospitals,
bombed village schools, the scattered
lemon-yellow cocoons at the bombed silk-factory,

and for the moment all my tears too
are used up, having seen today
yet another child with its feet blown off,
       a girl, this one, eleven years old,
patient and bewildered in her home, a fragile
small house of mud bricks among rice fields.

So I'll use my dry burning eyes
to photograph within me
dark sails of the river boats,
warm slant of afternoon light
apricot on the brown, swift, wide river,
village towers—church and pagoda—on the far shore,
and a boy and small bird both
perched, relaxed, on a quietly grazing
buffalo.   Peace within the
       long war.

It is that life, unhurried, sure, persistent,
I must bring home when I try to bring
the war home.
       Child, river, light.

Here the future, fabled bird
that has migrated away from America,
nests, and breeds, and sings,

common as any sparrow.

Denise Levertov

CHRISTMAS EVE

It's
  Been
    a
      Bleak
        December

With
      Nixon's
      B-52
        Bombers
          Bringing

Messages
  of
      Peace
        Peace
          Peace
            Peace
            Peace

and Hanoi goes up in flames
and I wonder what has
          happened
to my friends there.

Don Luce

AMERICA: DECEMBER 1972

The children
Have poured into the streets
Of our cities and villages
Students with hope for tomorrow
Join their grandparents' tiny tottering steps
To march, to sing, to stop the war

There comes a time
Writes Denise Levertov, the poet
When anger is the only love
And America debates the killing
Where do we channel our love
Dear friend Denise
Where?

Richard Nixon is the enemy
Not the people of Grinnell
Shout the angry students
On the evening of Nixon's
    declaration
    of war
    on the peoples of the world

Seven hundred
March at 2:00 a.m. that night
At Grinnell
A quiet flickering of candles
As defenseless and as
    strong as Gandhi
    with his spinning wheel

Peace Now!
Wrote the students at Drake
On the sidewalks of their campus
And were charged with
            Malicious
            Destruction
            Of Property
While Richard, the King
Dropped napalm on the
            children of Vietnam

Irresponsible dissent!
Cried ministers from their pulpits
Long-haired hippie radicals
Shouted politicians
Giving Fourth of July speeches
Months too early

We have become a dangerous country
Says Dan Ellsberg
Now charged with treason
For proving
Our country's leaders have been lying
For ten long years

Yes, out of this sea of anger/love
Respect for children will come
The bombing will stop
Because the children of America
      will no longer
      push the buttons
      that drop the bombs
      for Mr. Kissinger and
            Mr. Nixon.

Don Luce

from THE PEACEMAKER

The spark was struck, the flame was lit,
the fire danced in his eyes.
Man's power was in his grasp.
As the cold crept closer the flame was warmth,
as the darkness gnawed away the flame was cooking fire.
Around the fire's flickering fingers,
around its heat and light, the family gathered.
In its white heat, its yellow flames,
its blue darting shadows,
even in ashen coals,
the city was foretold.
A day when the pendulum would swing,
when time itself would serve this man,
when this huddled band of threatened men,
so awed by fire and rain,
would one day in their billions
live through the land
and threaten earth herself.

The fire of man,
that tiny flame
that fought with darkness for its life,
grows now beyond the man's control.
There is a swelling of the fire —
a pressure from within.
The inner flame heats the shell
until the force begins to build
and grow and swell again
and build and heat the outer skin
and still it grows,
this swelling cloud of fire
until it threatens all our lives.
How like a dangling sword
it hangs above our world
until all men turn to watch its turn
immobilized
transfixed
impaled upon this blade of fear and dread.
It is the weakness of man's strength.
It is failure at its peak.

Beneath the dangling sword
the nations rage and snarl and starve
while inept men debate the means of peace.

That mounting fire,
the coming stench,
like vapors from the deep
assail the nations,
transcend their borders
and rise to debase the nostrils of our God.
He abhors our wars,
our hate,
our violence.
It's not just hating war,
despising war,
sitting back and waiting for war to end.
It's not just loving peace,
wanting peace,
sitting back and waiting for peace to come.
Peace, like war, is waged.

Walker Knight

FOR A RUSSIAN

who broke thru a line of police in 1972 at a Moscow
shopping center to ask the visiting American Secretary of
State William Rogers to ''stop the killing;'' for those who
continue to ask; for those who answer with their lives.

Sandy Primm

FLOWER OF THE DRAGON

The most moving plea for peace I have ever heard was given by a young leader of the Vietnamese underground, Nguyen Hong Long.

I wish you could have known him as I did, but now he is gone, like the thousands of other Vietnamese who fought for freedom. In December of 1969 he tried to free the island concentration camp of Con Son, where there are thousands of political prisoners. His ship, the *Prajna*, was intercepted by a flotilla of Thieu's ships on the Mekong River. When the *Prajna* was seized, Long jumped on top of one of Thieu's gunboats and called for the soldiers of both sides to lay down their weapons and end the war themselves:

"War cannot continue without its supporters: to abolish war we only need to abolish the profession of soldiers, to refuse to bear arms and kill our brothers by command.

"Today, we eighteen fighters for peace, including Vietnamese and Americans, former ARVN soldiers and Communist guerrillas, having forgotten our past to live together as brothers, make the vow to march and spread the call for peace everywhere, until the war is ended. We march bearing broken guns and ringing bells made of cannon shells to call the stray soldiers to awaken from their slumber and abandon their murderous job; and to call the would-be soldiers to refuse to be drafted for the killing of their brothers.

"If the war ends and if peace comes, it is not because of Washington or Moscow, Paris or Peking, Hanoi or Saigon. It is because of you in the first instance. You create peace in your own hearts when you love all people and do not kill any man in any case, for any reason.

"We do not kill and peace has come to our hearts. We want that all of us may enjoy the same peace: therefore, we are willing to sacrifice ourselves, to suffer all hardships—imprisonment, torture, and even death—for our belief in the fraternity of man regardless of nationality, religion, race or ideology.

"The war-lovers hate us because they know that they are wrong. They call us draft-dodgers and evaders, deserters and betrayers. But the world knows that we are the first soldiers for a humanity without war, that we are the first soldiers in the last battle of man against the beast in himself.

"The authorities have a huge machine of coercion with their Police, Secret Service, Tribunal, Army, Prison. . . to force us into the profession of killing. Many young men dare not oppose that huge machine as individuals. Many others believe that military service is a sacred obligation. But day by day the number of conscientious objectors to all wars is increasing, and their solidarity around the world is becoming firmer and firmer. And day by day the truth of military service is evident to every man: a savage killing among human beings.

"Vietnam has suffered, more than any other country in the world, the curse of war. We aspire for peace more than any other people. Youth all over the world have demonstrated against the war. We have the greatest responsibility to struggle for peace with all our efforts and all our souls. We must turn the worst crime against humanity into the best dream of man realized on earth: the abolition of war.

"The Vietnamese believe strongly in the era of Long Hoa, the Flower of the Dragon, when the spiritual power in man shall overcome the brutal force in himself, when love shall overcome death, when peace shall overcome war. . ."

Long said that someday soldiers of both sides would see one another not as enemies but as brothers. If anything good comes out of this war, maybe it will be that.

"No matter what happens to me," he said, "or what happens to any of us, it doesn't matter. They can kill us all, but they can't kill an idea." When the Hoat Vu [Saigon secret police] took Long on Christmas Eve in 1969, I saw something in their faces while they were beating him. It was fear. You can chain a man's body, but you can't enslave his mind. The only prison is of the mind. If a man *feels* free, he *is* free.

When I saw Long's mother, I told her about the Flower of the Dragon. She had heard of the legend, but until then she had never understood it. The legend says that during the time of the dragon, the worst time for mankind, a small budding flower will spring up. And it will spread its petals throughout the world. It will be like a new evolution. Man will love and be free.

This is the eve of the Flower of the Dragon.

Richard Boyle

WINTER SOLDIERS

I have seen human hands
make peace signs
out of small windows
in a police van,
on their way to an unknown place,
unbeaten.
The future was unknown
but themselves they knew
the present they owned.

Donas John

WASHINGTON PROTEST [NIXON INAUGURAL]

Saturday, January 20, 1973

My wife and I march from the Lincoln Memorial to the Washington Monument. She has forgotten her gloves and puts her hands in my pockets when we stop. We march in the middle of the crowd where it is warmer. I see rosy-faced and avuncular looking Washington police manning the lines. They are not the Beasts. I see sailors with M.P. brassards, walking by two's, by the right flank march and they are out of sight. Those little white caps on their heads. They are not Beasts. The march is over and I can't stay for the speeches on the sloping mall. I can't stay. So up Fourteenth Street we go to Pennsylvania Avenue to wash against the police lines and the Military Police and I can see they are black young men from the ghettos and white young men from the corner stationary stores.

We can't get through the lines so we holler PEACE NOW, under the half-empty reviewing stands, holler at the one hundred and sixty shaven-legged drum majorettes and then at the five hundred horses (can we stampede them); the crowd in the reviewing stand is well dressed and disinterested. One thousand motorcycle cops pass by and the roar of their engines drown out our shouts.

We are turned back, politely and firmly. Go around to the Eighteenth Street, you can cross there, a policeman says. It's a cold day, isn't it, sir, he singles me out.

We go back down Fourteenth Street and now the Vietnam Vets Against the War are marching in, late, very late to join the main march.

They are coming in straggly lines, deliberately out of step, in pieces of uniforms, just kids, a children's crusade. They look so small, so young and they are brown and black and white. I want to cry and I can't. I see a taller veteran in sergeant's stripes leading a thin boy. The boy wears dark glasses and army pants, a blue windbreaker and he is resting his fingers lightly on the sergeant's arm as they walk along.

Lester Goldberg

CAPTIONS

The tortured welcome death in Viet Nam.
Folks *get that way* eating too much napalm.

The news reels.
The war rolls on.

In the Acid-yellow morning
small children open
(their crusted eyes)
to a symphony in blood.

The reels *CLICK*.
Death brings a certain calm.

After this,
gangly dogs patrol the streets.
They disregard
The Red Threat.
Only the children are left
for them to eat.

This is sickening.
We change the station.

In a stranger nation
students march with flowers for guns,
a balding angel
will appear
beneath a golden arch
and end the war
that no one had begun.
And the corpse of a country
lies riddled in half
And the fat little dogs
eat the treaty
and laugh.

Julie Robbins

FOOTNOTES TO PLATO # 2471

of the 4 human blessings the greatest is health
which is explicitly recognized by the rulers of the united states
        of america in this year 1974
who award the greatest boon within their power
free life long medical care
almost exclusively to soldiers & military veterans

it is proper in a state founded on a theory of perpetual war
to honor & benefit above all other classes of men and women
        soldiers & veterans
tell me who is it proper to honor & benefit above all others
in a state founded on a theory of perpetual peace

Sam Abrams

TET IN THE YEAR OF THE TIGER

The American public was brutally introduced to the word Tet on the last day of January 1968, when the Vietcong, in a series of daring attacks, carried the war from the distant rice fields into the streets and homes of South Vietnam, the backyard of the U.S. Embassy in Saigon and indirectly to the heart of Washington itself. For the second time in less than two centuries the land of Vietnam was shaken by violence during the New Year holiday. The first time was in 1789; in a surprise Tet offensive, the Vietnamese armies under Emperor Quang Trung, "the cotton-garbed, red-banner hero," the first Vietnamese socialist ruler, drove the Chinese Ch'ing occupation forces out of Thang Long ("Ascending Dragon," the ancient name of Hanoi).

But in normal times Tet, a mobile holiday corresponding to the new moon, occurring halfway between the winter solstice and the spring equinox (it falls this year on January 23), is the most cherished and important festival of the year. And naturally, the Vietnamese want to spend as much time as possible (officially three days but in reality one week) to enjoy it—or as the Vietnamese say, *An Tet*, to "eat" it; to immerse themselves in their traditional and national milieu, to refill themselves with physical and spiritual energies to face a year of struggle ahead. Tet, a unique Vietnamese combination of Thanksgiving, Christmas, New Year, Easter and Yom Kippur, embodies in its ceremonies as well as in its essence the whole concept of man and his place in the cosmos, his relations with the living, the dead and the spirits. It is a fascinating mixture of purifying Buddhism, edifying Confucianism and liberating Taoism, the three currents of religion and philosophy which have influenced the peculiar Vietnamese collectivist society since at least the beginning of the Christian era. Vietnamese Catholics are not immune to that delightful spiritual and philosophical harmonization either.

Tet is a yearly burst of Vietnamese romanticism and patriotism, nurtured in a rugged and beautiful land over centuries of hard work and bloody fighting. A Vietnamese may be a Marxist, an existentialist, a socialist, an anarchist or a militarist for the rest of the year, but when Tet comes, he reverts to his Vietnamese nature, as expressed in his joyful observance of an elaborate range of ceremonies. Most often he reveals it in poetry, which springs up as confidently as the buds in his garden. Indeed, Tet is a self-renewing Vietnamese poem, a poem written by a people who have learned how to be strong and sensitive, whose "pale fate" was to be the victims of the world's imperial powers, from the Mongols to the Americans, but whose unfulfilled hope is to live in peace with "all their brothers and sisters in the four seas."

This year Tet coincides with the first anniversary of the signing of the Paris agreement that was supposed to bring peace to Vietnam. But alas, the country's green mountains still resound to the crash of bombs, the limpid rivers are still devoid of singing passengers on pleasure boats, and the prisons are still crowded with people whose only crime was to cry aloud for peace. Let us hope that the Paris agreement will be fully implemented in the Year of the Tiger, that the physical and psychological prisoners of this too-long and too-cruel war will be freed to join the masses of Vietnamese peasants who have been chanting for centuries this optimistic and carefree song:

The first month of the year is for eating Tet at home
The second month is for gambling
And the third month is for going to the fairs.

During this Tet of the year of the Tiger, I am sure all Vietnamese would agree with the Swedish poet Erick Axel Karfeldt that "the greatest prayer of man does not ask for victory but for peace." Let us forget victory, let us live in concord and reconciliation so we Vietnamese can invite all our American friends to visit our land, to eat Tet with us, to gamble with our poets and to go to the fairs with our brave peasants.

Tran Van Dinh

FROM EAGLE TO SPRING

After over seven million tons of bombs, millions of dead and maimed, billions of dollars wasted, what is the result of the U.S. military intervention in Indochina? Laos is now two-thirds under Communist control, Cambodia, three-fourths. Before the U.S. armada rolled into South Vietnam, the country was non-Communist. The 1973 Paris Agreement, however, recognized the Vietcong as part of the national administrative structure and the North Vietnamese right to station troops in the South. Had Lao-tzu been a professor of political science at Harvard, he would advise the President in The Way of the Tao. He would "Counsel him not to use force to conquer the Universe, for this would only cause resistance. Thorn bushes spring up wherever the army has passed. Lean years follow in the wake of a great war and force is followed by loss of strength." He would suggest that "a great country is like a low land. It is the meeting ground of the Universe. The female overcomes the male with stillness, lying low in stillness. Therefore if a great country gives way to a smaller country, it will conquer the smaller country."

One of the official reasons for the U.S. military intervention in Indochina was the fear of Communism. How correct Lao-tzu was when he stated that "weapons are instruments of fear." Another reason was the attempt to change it into a democracy, U.S. style. Here again, The Master had a sound warning: "If you try to change it [the Universe] you will ruin it. If you try to hold it, you will lose it."

How could the Vietnamese, the Laotians and the Cambodians stand for so long against the huge American military power? Lao-tzu had a reply with which any serious student of wars of national liberation would agree: "He who stays where he is endures. To die but not to perish is to be eternally present."

Years from now I hope America will change its symbol from an eagle to a water spring. Because "under Heaven, nothing is more soft and yielding than water. Yet, for attacking the solid and strong, nothing is better." The U.S. will not need then billions for its military budget. When this is done, all the waters of the Mississippi, even of the Potomac will merge with those of the Ganges, of the Amazon, of the Nile, of the Niger, of the Mekong to flow into the high seas and to sing their song of everlasting harmony. We will surely have more than one generation of peace.

Tran Van Dinh

APPLICATION FOR DISCHARGE AS A CONSCIENTIOUS OBJECTOR

(1) 5 November, 1974

(2) William George Kelsey

(3) 157 44 2681

•

(7) United States Naval Academy, June 1969-June 1973

(8) No civilian employment after age 16

(9) Bancroft Hall, USNA, June 1969-June 1973
    NAS Cecil Field, Fla., July 1973-October 1973
    Training Command, Pensacola, Fla., November 1973-November 1974

•

(12 No application was made to the Selective Service System for classification as a conscientious objector prior to entry into the Armed Forces.

(13) Applicant has served more than 180 days in the naval service.

(14) It is my firm conviction that I cannot and will not take part in any war. I further can no longer allow my energies and abilities to be used in serving in and maintaining an organization which has no constructive purpose on this planet. Arguments concerning the validity of our military in terms of national defense have become pointless with the development of nuclear technology. A war releasing the destructive potentials of the Superpowers would result in the certain extinction of most forms of life on the earth.

Even "limited" wars involving the use of so-called conventional weapons leave scars which last longer than the memory of the issues over which battles are fought. The land of Indochina may never recover its original ecological balance; unexploded ordnance will continue to detonate well after our lifetimes; and the suffering there extends to the yet unborn—for many Vietnamese mothers now give birth to deformed infants who are victims of chromosome damage done by the presence of defoliants in the food chain.

I am fascinated by the languages, customs, lifestyles, and ethnologies of the various peoples of the earth. The study of their histories, problems, and conflicts absorbs much of my time. In my travels I have found that I love Life and that I love this world too much to be a contributor to its damage or possible end.

There is much to be studied, much to be learned, but I feel that I can say with confidence that many of the world's governments, including that of the United States, are travelling in a disasterous direction. Having communicated well with foreigners of numerous ideologies and religions I cannot accept the right of the state (or trust in its ability) to choose my friends and my enemies for me.

I have no illusions as to my ability to change the present state of affairs. However I do believe that this decision is a small step in the right direction.

(15) Central to the initial development of my beliefs has been the Palestine conflict. I was brought face-to-face with the reality of war at the age of four when my parents moved into a house in a refugee camp on the outskirts of Amman, Jordan. My early childhood friends and playmates were uprooted Palestinians who had been driven from their homes in what is now Israel. The scenes of the camp haunt me to this day and the ethos of the displaced person is a feeling that I cannot help but share. This consciousness is one that binds me to the oppressed in all corners of the earth. The hunger of any person is my hunger; the struggle of the exploited is my struggle; and the ecstasy of the liberated is my ecstasy.

I was brought up as a Christian by my Conservative Baptist missionary parents. This upbringing was characterized by much religious study, Bible reading, and church attendence.

While attending high school in Beirut, Lebanon I saw the ships of the Sixth Fleet visiting port and was impressed. My final two years of high school were spent in Blackwood, New Jersey. While there I applied for and was accepted by the Naval Academy. At the time it seemed like a most valid course of action, but it may have been the result of subconscious desire to affirm my identity as an American.

I entered the Naval Academy as a rather conservative teenager, believing in and supporting the war effort in Southeast Asia. My knowledge and understanding of the Middle East were in conflict with many policies of the government. I did not see a contradiction in my role, believing that I had a duty to remain in the service while writing and speaking the truth.

Wanting to learn Chinese I chose Far Eastern Affairs as my major. This, and countless other influences put me in a position where I was actively questioning the war and by First Class year I was bitterly opposed to it. My final project at the Academy was a lengthy research into the political and military relationship of the United States with the Meo tribespeople of Laos. In the Conclusion I accused the highest authority of crimes against humanity and of deceiving the American people.

Relieved by the withdrawal of U.S. forces from Indochina and what was supposed to be the end of American involvement, I accepted my Commission in good faith. In November of 1973 I arrived in Pensacola to commence flight training. Even at this time I was aware that I was compromising my true beliefs and was forced to rationalize my role to myself and to others. Knowing from experience in Jordan the effects of attack aircraft on civilians (i.e. their inability to select military targets with accuracy, the use of napalm, etc.), I chose to fly helicopters, thinking of the possibility of doing rescue work.

It was not long before I realized that I was still concerned and unhappy with what I was doing. Many sleepless nights were spent contemplating this crisis and I often found it difficult to concentrate on my flying duties. On one occasion I had lunch with a Cambodian student who poured out his feelings to me on the war in his country and the traumatic effects it was having on his family and himself. He had no desire to fight for the Lon Nol government or the United States as a mercenary but feared a court martial if he were to drop the flight program. I was so disturbed and outraged by the situation that I flew a totally unsatisfactory hop that afternoon.

What I have presented is only a basic sketch of my philosophical development and some major events in my life. However I consider each day a new chance to grow, to learn, and to search for Truth within one's self and within the Universe. This search includes reading of which I do much. Books that have influenced me include a variety dealing with history, religion, and philosophy. I am particularly concerned with exploring the roots and causes of war—among them ignorance, hate, racism, exploitation, militarism, and national chauvinism. Also important have been discussions with various individuals I have met on the road. All encounters influence a person somewhat and it is important to learn something from each. It would be impossible to list all the people who have taught me something, but they include professors, Vietnam veterans, soldiers of many armies, and occasional political exiles.

(16) The distance from the idea to the act is often long and sometimes difficult. So has it been for me. One of my greatest problems was in making the decision to drop from the flight program. It is not easy to quit, and I would not have felt completely satisfied had I acted while under pressure at Whiting Field. While on leave, far from Pensacola, and while calm, happy, and with friends, I came to the conclusion that the time had come to stop.

I have decided that from henceforth my every act must be constructive and meaningful to myself and to others. No longer will I be a cog in what I consider to be a parasitic and lethal machine. I have committed myself to pacifism and will carry out this commitment in every sense of the word. This firm state of mind is best expressed by the Hindi word *dharma* which describes individual conduct in conformity to the ultimate Truths of the cosmos.

(17) I can think of few instances in which I would be justified in the use of force. Naturally I cannot predict my emotional reaction to every situation. If I were to be confronted with a madman or a drunk who threatened myself or people nearby I might be justified in using violence as a last resort to restrain him.

I do recognize that many historical situations have arisen in which pacifism became impractical if not absurd. Such cases would include that of a Jew confronted with the Gestapo or a Palestinian faced with an Israeli soldier evicting him from his land. An exploited and oppressed African may have no alternative other than violence in his efforts to rid himself of colonial rule. It is the duty of the pacifist to oppose the causes of war as well as war itself. By speaking out actively against repression and various forms of injustice a cohesive anti-war movement could help prevent potentially violent situations from arising and through boycotts and passive resistance perhaps dismantle an already existing situation of this kind.

The death penalty I oppose, even for the worst of war criminals. People learn and change, and others can learn from those who have made mistakes. *Inside the Third Reich* was written by Albert Speer, the chief architect and armaments minister for Adolf Hitler. Convicted and sentenced at the Nuremburg trials, he was able to write his memoirs after spending twenty years in Spandau prison. During this time he had the opporunity to reflect upon his role in the Nazi regime and its consequences. Speer's observations concerning responsibility for war crimes and man's misuse of technology are most profound.

(18) My daily life style has changed somewhat with my decision to apply for a discharge as a conscientious objector. The resolution of a crisis has made me happier, more sure of myself and more prepared to confront the future. As I write this application I am inspired by the ecstasy of being alive and I hope to take this attitude with me through the upcoming proceedings. . . .

William G. Kelsey

A DIFFERENT DRUM

Give me the banner stained with blood;
I'll bury it with a sigh,
    to the beat of a muffled drum.
Give me the flag that flies a dove,
I'll free it to the sky.
    to the beat of a different drum.

Give me the pennons bullet-frayed,
I'll post them side by side,
    to the beat of a battle drum
until the colors merge and fade
in ribbons wind has tied
    to the beat of a different drum.

Flag me a crescent, stripe and star
with eagle, cross and sun
    to muffle the battle drums,
then hear me sing a new hurrah
for colors all in one,
    to the beat of a different drum;
    the heart is a lovely drum.

Miriam C. Maloy

STANDING LIKE THE END OF WAR

The mountain was more
of the dark she had been sure of
all day.
She was stuck on its side
unable to move up or down
and the clouds which had closed in that morning
hung greyly over her imbalance.
The drama of the death she imagined
was thwarted by her isolation: who would see?
She forced herself up,
up the rocks to the top where she saw nothing
through her dripping eyes.
She started down the gentler slope.

The deer walked into the clearing
and stopped. She waited for the others —
one, two came beside the first. They stayed.
They swayed like young saplings.
Three deer and one person,
standing like a dream of peace.

Annie Stine

HOA BINH

We watch the news reports and look for the faces of friends, for farmers we drank rice wine with, for students we swapped languages with. We can smell the sweat of refugees crowded together, hear the bombs in the distance, and feel the dry season sun on the back of our necks. As the saga began to unfold we cried, oh no, not again, for Christ's sake not again.

But now *Hoa Binh*. Peace. It's all over. It's finally, finally over.

When I was an IVS volunteer in Vietnam *hoa binh* seemed to be something Vietnamese waited for, longed for, sang songs about, but never really expected to come. Peace had a fairy tale quality to it; it was like the pot of gold that lies at the end of the rainbow in our stories, like Snow White awakened by the charming prince. "My land," a girl student from DaNang wrote in a composition, "is a place where peace never comes," where "the word peace means the same with a fairy in the fairy tale my grandmother tells me." Peace had become something one invoked—like a god. And like a god, it was something miraculous and when it came, as Trinh Cong Son sang, even "the stones would break out in song."

John C. Schafer

IVS: International Voluntary Services

188

INVITATIONS

We will invite the youth
   Who bear on their bodies
   And in their minds and hearts
      the sounds of war.
   The brothers from the Chinese border
      to the Gulf of Thailand.

We will invite our friends
   from the West.
   Those whose fathers went
      and never returned.
   Those whom the war has taken
      their loved ones.

We will invite our friends
   from north and south Korea,
   From east and west Germany,
   And the poor miserable ones
      from Santo Domingo.

We will invite the survivors
   From behind the mushroom
      columns of smoke
   of Hiroshima and Nagasaki.

We will invite the demonstrators
      against war
   And the mothers from five continents.
   Our own mothers in traditional dress
      and long hair
   Will welcome these suffering
      people from all over.

We will say new words
   Our hearts filled with human love
   And a new language
   For those who were the enemy.

Hai Ha

THRENODY FOR A REVOLUTIONARY
TERRY F. ROBBINS, 1948-1970

My poems had failed
    planes bombed & strafed
        that night
    children & old men shrieked
        their deepest agonies

Your piercing scream
as the atoms of your body
        blasted to wind & elements
            fire becoming air
            blood-splotched wall charred

My poems couldn't compete/with TV or movies
        weren't cathartic enough for the colonels & generals
            to distract their thinking
            to entertain their thoughts

Northern Ohio in May
flowers give their first bloom
Blond, small-budded girl
    shoves daisy up pronging rifle

(It is night
my poem is a lie!
their napalm was truth
        that night)

It is day
her jugular slashed by a bullet
    blood gushing
        screaming panic…

2.

The phone rings
(It is late May
        & humid)
your partisans identified you
(Last February
reading the *Chicago Tribune* in Miami
        photograph of a movie actor
           running from his Village townhouse
           clutching a canvas
        the gap on 11th Street
a home/your bomb factory
        shattered)

The FBI could never identify your carcass
You must have been too close to the explosion
        never one for details
        four years before when we shared a room at Kenyon
            you, the pacifist
                    fighting me over a girl
                    realizing your violence
                    later

when you saw a man die
            in the slums of Cleveland
as the bullet plunged into his brain
        he jerked in shock
            falling to the ground
            writhing uncontrollably
When they put him into the meat wagon
after seeing them wipe up his blood
        you proclaimed the right of the revolution
                your right
                to kill
                    Killer!
Your comrades announce your obituary
        with a warning:
"Death to the fascist insect/that preys on the people!"

                3.

It is May again
the fifth May of the poem
        this artifice of reality
        this buttress of life
                which attempts to construct meaning
                    out of the trash heap of history

Saigon fell 6 days ago
            the last day of April, 1975
My poems had succeeded
        to bring life
        to save life
        to create an alternative life
                to that madness
                    (a child hugging her decapitated mother)
but there was no joy
        only the confusing smog of history
            your failure to survive...

Geoffrey Cook

OUR SOLE NOURISHMENT IS HOPE

Peter Stool died from cancer on the first day of spring 1975 at age 28. Having survived the killing ground in Indochina, much of which was defoliated by toxic herbicides since suspected of causing cancer and birth defects, he lived in Jersey City, N.J., was active in Vietnam Veterans Against the War, and one day learned he might never see the end of the war. The following passages are from his hospital diary:

13 Dec. '74
Friday the thirteenth!...In some ways I am lucky. If I am told I have six months to live, then I have six months of living which I can do free of the addictions and chains of surface realities. On the other hand I might not have had cancer and I might have spent the next six months wrapped in my neuroses and ruled by trivia, and then had a steel safe fall on my head or be struck by lightning. In which case would I be luckier? I am finally aware (in a more than intellectual sense) that of course it's not the count of my days, but their measure one by one, that gives meaning to my life. Nothing comes easy...

16 Dec. '74
Last night's dreams were restless and angry, pre-tumor types in which I rage at all those things I can't change. Perhaps the inactivity has upset me. I've done nothing for five days and I'm almost looking forward to tomorrow's arteriogram. The waiting wears me down on a sublevel hard to reach, its effects are subtle. This whole trip reminds me more and more of Vietnam, except I know that in the end I get it.

23 Dec. '74

Went into the treatment room and he gave me a local but I guess I was on an express cause I felt the whole thing, from this needle bite into the skin and the grind into the bone and soon I was hanging on to the end of the table knowing if I moved I would twist like a worm cut in half. The pain was incredible, even the nurses felt sorry for me, and when it was over I just lay on the tabble with my legs vibrating fast, as my body caught up to what had happened, and then I got up and walked back to my room. I lay down on the bed and suddenly tears were pouring from my eyes and breath just gulped in and out like I had run a mile on one foot…Thinking of all the soldiers who have died with legs blown off, before morphine and the like, all who were left to die scattered in heaps on every hill on the face of the earth. All the useless lies, all the ideals, all the honor; somehow none of this matters much when weighed against people dying so stupidly.

Our sole nourishment is hope,
and we spend our meager supply
in vain attempts to make our mirages permanent.
Will we ever be one with each other,
will we cease to grasp and clutch in our greed?
Can we but see the vast golden fields of grain
that wave within us all;
then we would make our lives happy, and would fear nothing,
strong in the bounty of humanity.
We are miraculous creatures all,
waiting to discover our own beauty.

Peter Stool

WITH PEACE COMES REALITY

"We have not urged the French to negotiate with Ho Chi Minh, even though he probably is supported by a considerable majority of the Vietnamese people, because of his record as a Communist. . . .Ho Chi Minh is the strongest and perhaps the ablest figure in IndoChina and any suggested solution which excludes him is an expedient of uncertain outcome." (State Department Policy Statement—Sept. 27, 1947)

I share with more than 2½ million other American men and women a somewhat dubious honor. We were all participants in this country's first losing war—Vietnam.

Twenty-five painful years have passed since the first American commitment of $10 million to the French war effort. Vietnam, the country Charles DeGaulle called "le pays pourri" (the rotter country), has finally found the peace so long denied it.

Vietnam was, for those who served there, an experience none of us will soon forget. It has been said that no one ever leaves Vietnam and with this I surely agree, as I have now been home for close to six years and seem unable, perhaps unwilling, to forget.

Not everything experienced in a war is either traumatic or even exciting. There are probably more boring times than memorable ones, yet, in spite of this, war can often be a very attractive adventure. We should never underestimate the opportunity for enjoyment in the spectacle it provides, the simple pleasures of comradeship and the ever present delight in destruction that are an everyday part of war. But for every delight, there was a corresponding horror and it was the horror that has stayed with me longer than any momentary delight.

One's feelings about Vietnam can never be simply described in terms of black and white. During the last five years I have been delicately balancing between bitterness about having had to serve in a war few wanted and so many tried to avoid and genuine pleasure for having had the chance to be part of what has become my greatest adventure.

More than any other experience in my life, Vietnam is responsible for the opinions and outlooks that guide me today.

Most importantly, Vietnam taught me that Americans are just like everyone else: no better, sometimes worse. What discernible difference is there between Germans or Japanese war criminals who argued that they were just obeying orders and Lt. Calley, who mouthed the same plea?

Gone was my idealistic notion that Americans were something special, somehow motivated by utopian desires for a better world. It's ironic that we find ourselves in the midst of the bi-centennial celebration of the Revolutionary War, yet we have spent the last 25 years crushing revolutions around the world.

It was Lyndon Johnson, who in 1964 promised not to send American boys to die in Southeast Asia, yet less than four years later I found myself in that very same Southeast Aisa he promised to keep me out of.

I went off to war, believing what I was being ordered to do was best for my country. I never once suspected that MY President was lying to me. I fell hook, line and sinker for the standard patriotic line and worked hard to attain our stated goal—a viable non-Communist Vietnam.

Seven years later I find myself asking a question I could never have dared to think about while I was serving in Vietnam—Could we win the war?

After quite a bit of soul searching I'm convinced the answer is no. The question of victory, however, remains academic as there was never anything to win.

The trail of American support for Indochina is studded with tragedy. Americans saw the war through a glass darkly, if at all.

As an advisor, I worked closely with the South Vietnamese and their utter apathy convinced me that all the money in the world could never buy the willingness needed to fight the kind of war necessary to defeat the Communists. We were, quite simply, on the wrong side.

Some critics maintain that if the military had been given a free hand, the war would have ended in victory. The politicians, they contend, tied the generals' hands.

We lost in Vietnam because we never had the support of the people. Thus, the most vital element in this war was never ours. The Communists realized this and as a result won the all important political war, which eventually lead to military victory.

Who lost the war in Vietnam? For years to come this will be as hotly argued a question as who lost China. Already strident voices attempt to lay the "blame" on Congress, threatening to take us back to the anti-Communist recriminations of the early and mid 50s.

Richard Nixon repeatedly vowed that he would not be the first American President to lose a war. Yet somehow, inexorably we lost. He does not, of course, share the blame alone. He shares it with five other American Presidents from Truman to Ford. He also shares it with the American people, who stood by and allowed a succession of Presidents and Congresses to draw us ever further into this doomed war.

Will America learn the lessons of this lost war? Can we turn defeat into victory by admitting that the Vietnam war was never ours to win? Will it stand as a lesson for future Presidents, that never again will a majority of Americans permit such a war?

Perhaps what we really need is an end to the recriminations. Vietnam was the watershed in my life, as it taught me more than I ever believed possible. it awakened me to the fallibility of America. Let us learn from the ashes of this war and heed the words of Arthur Schlesinger: "It is not only idle but unfair to seek out guilty men. . . The Vietnam story is a tragedy without villains."

Peter Berenbak

EXORCISM

Goodbye   old war   Saigon whore
      VD   VC   MARINES   with maps
         on helmets   mass graves
                putrid bodies

Goodbye   B-52's   and three columns of
    bombs for support   pocked fields   burning
         monks   Nobel-peace-prize smiles
                fourteen years

Goodbye   body-counts   bandaged
         prisoners   too many beers

      a night   Mekong jungle rot
                napalmed kids

            hello   america

Frank Finale

NIGHTMARES

When it comes to me
it slithers
    creeps
    crawls to my memory
and it doesn't seem to care about the agony in it's footsteps

My body shivers: it knows this ghoul
so many, many times it has come to me

My mind flees to dark corners
and hides
from the thoughts of the terror
and the cold damp dreams
rancid with fear, anger
rank with putrid, foul death

bits of blood run down my face
shreds of life
that were not mine
but were
from the community of man

and the lives
wave and wander in my dreams:
"For us!"
"Did we not live?"
"Tell us why!"

James D. Lange

HOPE

I hope they understand
that I cannot recall their names
I hope they understand
that is futile for me to try

And in those late nights
when too much drink
strips away my shield of concern for the outer world
and I fall back into that other world
stored in black-borders
and the tears flow
across my mouth
and choke my voice
and I shake with sorrow
after four years, No! five now
away from that place

I hope my wife understands
though I know she is terrified of me like this
I hope she understands
that I cannot say
I simply cannot
about what it was like over there
who they were
or why they died

and hope that she lets me cry into my sleep
my sleep with dreams of rotten hell
        that I care not to, could never, share with another
So I might wake, now sober, now drained
and wonder
and wipe those skeletons that cling
the horror I face in those nights
away
        and shove the musty bones
of outrageous guilt or fear or hate
back to their cellar

and pray they will not return
knowing without doubt
that I will carry them with me
until I die

and perhaps even after

James D. Lange

VOICES AT A CONVENTION

take another drink, fear has fled;
don your good ole legion cap
and toast the good ole dead.
hear the voices,
noises, laughs. (dont hear the chorus:
drown it out
with shout.)

1st voice:
sure, i was in combat;
my wing bombed 'em to hell and gone.
'course, now, i am a very gentle person...

>   chorus:
>   killing isnt killing
>   when it isnt face to face?

2nd voice:
i just dont understand
cowards. yellow punks, oughta shoot em!

>   chorus:
>   have you forgotten what
>   "keep a tight one" means?
>   or were you ever close enough
>   to learn?

3rd voice:
yeah, yeah. it was ok, i guess.
but when i think of all
my buddies, well, i just dont
know what to think.

>   chorus:
>   think of relief. it was
>   your buddy, brother, son;
>   it wasn't you.

4th voice:
God! we ripped right on through!
like shit through a horn!
Jesus! the sights ive seen!!

> chorus:
> did you see the flower
> trying to grow
> out of the putrefaction?
> tank treads dont care
> about bodies or flowers.

nothing is all bad.
except some things.

Hillman Taylor

VETERAN

Two wars old, relic
of another time,
oblivious, uncoping,
hoary as his memories,
never living—
only reliving.

Ed White

OUT TO PASTURE

Rumbling sounds surround you
    as you tread the grass below
    advancing on the imaginary foe

for honor
       in love
    to remember the sacrifice

O rusted reason
   your cannon is a compass needle now
       pointing to the west
       where the sun sets on
   your iron willed weathered worn ways

   black tongues
        prostrate
     before the pleasure packed packages
       darting past
   your last gasp for history

   perhaps in our time
   herds of your breed
        antiquated by nurturing hearts
     could be sent out to pasture
     a resting place
    for memories and birds

Cliff Catton

AMNESTY

Let them come home, those sons,
to their anxious mamas and papas,
to wipe away their tears,
so they may see their child in adulthood,
before their lives are over.

Let them return, those husbands and boyfriends
to their waiting wives and lovers
to start to live and love again.
Death will separate them soon enough.

Let them be fathers
to their confused children
that they have never seen or known
before the children are grown
without having had a father.

Let them come, those who fled,
back to our bleeding nation
and let the wound be healed
before it is too late.

Let them live again,
they who were too brave,
who loved and cared too much
to let a government force them
to kill another human being.

Please, let them come home.

Linda Kay Vanderberg

MARKING TIME

Two flags on the Peace Bridge
two flags in the October air.
A river that spans the boundary
between countries, between freedom & prison.

Photographers rush forward, TV cameramen
point microphones, questions.
US marshalls wait to take their prisoner,
the one clear eye will bring it all back.

Two flags flying on the Peace Bridge,
we are walking Bruce Byer home.
Home from his war, his exile in Canada.

I want to say that it was yesterday,
but two years have passed.
Somewhere in Buffalo he gets out of jail,
turns to face a new set of charges,
another courtroom.

This is what remains, these reasons
that smoulder unnoticed,
here in the land of victory.

Gerald McCarthy

AMNESTY?

We are a country that cannot now be easily described or understood. Speaking endlessly of peace and our longing to have it, we make sure the Vietnamese and the Cambodians do not enjoy it. Speaking endlessly of honor and duty, we neglect and ignore veterans of the Viet Nam war. Speaking endlessly of our wealth and technology, we seek the perfected B-1 bomber, not to help 23 million Americans below the poverty level last year. Speaking endlessly of morals and of courage, we offer nothing to the war resisters and deserters but an insulting and stupid scheme to get them back.

The hammer blows begin to fall on us: there is inflation, unemployment, an energy crisis, crime. The country that thought it should save South Viet Nam, and teach it to be a democracy, has been flawed and poisoned by Watergate. It is we who need to be taught, not the Vietnamese. The country that spent $120 billion on the war in Indochina has no jobs for five and a half million people, including over 300,000 Vietnam-era veterans out of work. The country that so fears being cold, or short of gas, does not remember now that a B-52 uses 2,300 gallons of fuel per hour, that 65 million gallons must have been used in the 1972 Christmas bombing of Hanoi and Haiphong.

We do not have much to be proud of except for those among us who did not yield, did not compromise, did not collaborate. There were very young men who defied the old men by refusing to go to war. How odd it is that those Americans who would not sweep the villages of Viet Nam, who would not do the killing or make the killing possible, are the ones to be punished. No one has suggested that Rostow, McNamara, Bunker, Huntington, Westmoreland, Rusk, Humphrey do alternate service. Instead President Ford, a man whose heart is on the football field, has tried to heal our wounds. But he does not see the wounds and cannot measure them. The men who left rather that go to war have not come back in large numbers. The so-called amnesty plan is a failure; in Washington, D.C. they are surprised. Of course. The truth is that the resisters and deserters know that America still has not changed. They do not need their country any more. It is America that so urgently, so sadly, has need of them.

Gloria Emerson

ATROCITY

William Niederland, a psychiatrist in New York who has worked with survivors of the Nazi holocaust since 1945, once began a lecture on the concentration camp survivor syndrome by saying "I am here to speak to you about matters of great sadness."

We are here to talk about matters of great sadness.

One evening last week, while working on this conference, I heard about a Viet Nam veteran who revealed during his work with a therapist that among 140 Vietnamese he killed in Viet Nam, there were 34 children, whom he machine-gunned by accident. He estimates they were all under 10 years of age. When I heard this I stopped writing and tried to think about the event. I was overcome with what felt like endless horror and a feeling of hopelessness. How could I or anyone be helpful to that person, how could anyone ultimately acknowledge his humanity, in the face of such a terrible act? I despaired of ever being able to relate to him.

I thought then of all the Viet Nam veterans who live with the memories of similar cruelty, and wait too for someone to help them return to civilized living. I wondered how this program can possibly deal with all that confronts it. There seemed to be no point, and I thought perhaps we would all be better off not trying. After a time spent in this vein of despair and hopelessness, I noticed the dates of the man's tour in Viet Nam. They were about the same as mine. Because of other data, and without much stretch of the imagination, it became clear to me that I may well have seen this man in Viet Nam for a therapeutic interview or two, and, as a result, he may have been helped to return to duty, and, the next week, or month, or whenever, kill the children.

Strange as it may seem, that thought has helped me a great deal. It has helped me see once again the most essential truth about how we are trying to help ourselves and each other: we are doing it because we are all in this together. Most obviously, all of us who were there; but everyone else too, who worked to earn the money to pay the tax to buy the gun and ammunition, and the airplane and the fuel which got the soldier there. Every American taxpayer paid an average of $3300 for the Viet Nam war. If you don't yet quite see how connected you were, eventually you will.

Arthur S. Blank, Jr.

THE BODY COUNT BOX SCORE

We begin with the premise
that the words contain magic,
since they do not contain reason,
wisdom, or meaning.

And the magic claims a priesthood,
not chosen but elect.

With the glad brave
self-sacrifice of youth
we gave ourselves up
and wrote ourselves off.

Well, some of us came back,
have been back, in fact, for years,

fascinated unto autism
by the intense text of silence

to our credit.

For you,
we murdered guilt.

Tom Hawkins

I WENT SO I COULD SAY I KNEW

I went, did my duty, and didn't volunteer. For the whole year full of days I tried not to count, my anger hardened into steel. When the others grumbled, I set my jaw in silence; when they went berserk, I turned away; and when I saw the dead carried in plastic bags, I did not say I told you so. Through it all I stuck to my convictions. There were times I was afraid, when I really *saw* them in the bush, but I never once fired my weapon because I had no quarrel with them. And when, in my final minute there, I saw the land through a yellow haze recede from view behind the safety of a cloud, I knew not only that I had endured but that I had been right all along. I knew this because I had seen the villages we passed through and what we did to the people there, and the holes we flushed or burned them out of, and the stares of the people there whose eyes spoke silent resistance and of a patience longer than memory. I had seen too the whores in Saigon. I knew that my only justification for going was to see all this first-hand, so that I could say I *knew*.

I knew too that I couldn't go back home. They greeted me at the airport, mother more full of tears now than before, as if sure now that she had lost me forever, and father with a half-smile confirming his suspicion that this was a dirty little war merely. And Jane, twelve now, not running out to me, but hiding, almost cowering, behind my mother's skirts as if I were a stranger.

So after the welcome home I packed my things and moved to another part of the city. I took odd jobs and returned to the university, standing silent in the crowds during the spring protests and seeing only greying glimpses now of the yellow country—of an old man pushing a handcart left in the dust of a passing jeep, of a swarm of copters hovering like dragonflies over a distant hill until one of them suddenly fell out of the sky like a heavy stone, and always of the faces in Saigon in which there lurked cats about to spring even as the faces went stolidly about their business. No one asked me if I had been there and no one asked me to speak, but I stood there with the rest of the crowd voting with my body and sometimes seeing then for the first time what my eyes had really seen.

Emilio De Grazia

from "Little Sister Death"—a short story

LETTER

to a north Vietnamese soldier
whose life crossed paths with mine
in Hue. February 5th, 1968.

Thought you killed me
with that rocket? Well, you nearly did:
splattered walls and splintered air,
knocked me cold and full of holes,
and brought the roof down on my head.

But I lived,
long enough to wonder often
how you missed; long enough
to wish too many times
you hadn't.

What's it like back there?
It's all behind us here;
and after all those years of possibility,
things are back to normal.
We just had a special birthday,
and we've found again our inspiration
by recalling where we came from
and forgetting where we've been.

Oh, we're still haggling over pieces
of the lives sticking out
beyond the margins of our latest
history books; but no one haggles
with the authors.

Do better than that,
you cockeyed gunner with the brass
to send me back alive among a people
I can never feel
at ease with any more:

remember where you've been, and why.
and then build houses;
build villages, songs and children,
dikes and schools; build
communion in that green land
I blackened with my shadow
and the shadow of my flag.

Remember Ho Chi Minh
was a poet: please,
do not let it all
come down to nothing.

W.D. Ehrhart

209

DANCING

Having been where contrasts meet,
I perceive reality to be
Whatever looms largest in the mind.

Thus truths are never absolute;
Nebulous, they never lose the shifting
Beat of music changing time.

Books I read, and faces seen
In sunlight tell me where I am;
At night, this truth melts away;

An older truth looms within
And I submit, take my rifle,
Rejoin comrades on patrol

Until the sun returns the books,
And faces, and the other truth
I dance with to a kinder beat.

W.D. Ehrhart

from A CONFIRMATION
for Gerry Gaffney,
a good friend in a bad time

Solemn Douglas firs stride slowly
down steep hills to drink
the waters of the wild Upper Umqua.
In a small clearing in the small
carved ravine of a feeder stream
we camp, pitching our tent
in the perfect stillness of the shadows
of the Klamath Indians. Far off,
almost in a dream, the logging trucks
growl west down through the mountains
toward the mills in Roseburg.

I hold the stakes, you hammer—
"Watch the fingers!"—both laughing.
Both recall, in easy conversation,
one-man poncho tents rigged
side by side in total darkness;
always you and I, in iron heat,
in the iron monsoon rains—
not like this at all; and yet,
though years have passed
and we are older by a lifetime,
a simple slip of thought, a pause,
and here: nothing's changed.

For we were never young, it seems;
not then, or ever. I couldn't even cry
the day you went down, screaming, jagged
angry steel imbedded in your knee—
I knew you would live,
and I knew you wouldn't be back,
and I was glad, and a little jealous.
Two months later I went down.

We all went down eventually,
the villages aflame, the long
grim lines of soldiers, flotsam
in the vortex of a sinking illusion:
good-bye, Ginny; good-bye, John Kennedy;
good-bye, Tom Paine and high school history—
though here we are still, you and I.
We live our lives now
in a kind of awkward silence
in the perfect stillness of the shadows
of the Klamath Indians.

And I am genuinely happy
to be with you again. We stand
on the rocks; you point to clear
patches between white water
where the shadows of sleek fish slip,
effortless streaks of energy.
I'm clumsy: with an old, eager patience
you teach me how to cast the fly
gently, so it rides on the surface
with the current, far downstream—
till the rod bends, springs back,
bends again: strike! Your excitement
rises above the river like a wild
song the Douglas firs bend
imperceptibly to hear: shouts,
advice, encouragement, half an hour
and a fourteen-inch rainbow trout
panting hard, eyes alive, its tiny heart
beating with defiance still unbroken
though I hold the fish
helpless in my hands.

I throw the fish back
in the awkward silence, and you
slip your arm around my shoulders
gently for a moment, knowing why.

W.D. Ehrhart

THE TEACHER
(*Sandy Spring Friends School, September, 1978*)

A cold moon hangs
cold fire among the clouds,
and I remember colder nights
in hell when men died
in such pale light as this
of fire swift
and deadly as a heart of ice.

Hardly older then
than you are now,
I hunched down shaking
like an old man
alone in an empty cave
among the rocks of ignorance
and malice honorable men
call truth.

Out of that cave I carried
anger like a torch
to keep my heart from freezing,
and a strange new thing called
love
to keep me sane.

A dozen years ago,
before I ever knew you,
beneath a moon not unlike
this moon tonight,
I swore an oath to teach you
all I know—
and I know things
worth knowing.

It is a desperate future
I cling to,
and it is yours.
All that I have lived for
since that cold moon long ago
hangs in the balance—
and I keep fumbling for words,
but this clip-clapper tongue
won't do.

I am afraid;
I do not want to fail:

I need your hands to steady me;
I need your hearts to give me courage;
I need you to walk with me
until I find a voice that speaks
the language
that you speak.

W.D. Ehrhart

CAVE DWELLERS
*(at the Association of the U.S. Army Weapons Exhibition,
Washington, DC, October, 1978)*

A hundred and thirty people gather outside:
pacifists, life-long Quakers, Iranian students,
a small contingent of Cypriots —
and our two dozen high   school kids
off from school, full of adventure,
curious.
Only a few
familiar faces here: the old pros,
gaunt, as always; greeting my own
familiar face with old
sad eyes.

We march on the sidewalk.
We carry signs:
        "Stop the Merchants of Death."
        "Feed the Cities, Not the Pentagon."
A boy with a trumpet plays taps.

All day long, limosines and taxis,
green government buses roll by,
windows closed.
Policemen sip coffee.

Inside, a hundred
million dollars changes hands:
helicopters, rocket-launchers, tanks
change hands like beach balls,
pots and pans.

Outside, a hundred
tired pickets scramble for shelter
from the rain — and after all
these years, at last I know
the war is over, the few survivors
scattered to the hills
to live in caves.

W.D. Ehrhart

THE LAST DAY

Night drifts coldly into dawn.
Stark slate turns
first grey, then red.
The sea lies flat;
the hills lie breathless.

Terror and alarm, confusion,
fire, death, apocalyptic change—
all these we imagined.
In the darkest alleys of our minds
we covered every possibilty.

No one thought of this.

The sun climbs in the east;
still the streets and roads
are empty. No one moves;
each is locked forever

in a dream.

W.D. Ehrhart

PAX

Mrs. Smith, old widow
with her television loaded
with big colored pictures
of grandchildren--
burn her up.
This is the national defense.

It is necessary. History
forced our hand. Our honor
is at stake, our national place.

Michael Grady Maxwell,
fourth grade shortstop
with knee patches and
a d-plus in math,
cremate him alive,
an acceptable loss.

Diplomacy and wealth,
the day-to-day feeling
that we are unsafe,
seeing our beliefs pushed
too long and too far
into the mud.

The Umanoff family,
the father a leather worker
wife a brick mason,
six children in steps
with wide trusting smiles.
Reduce them to ash
sucked up nine thousand feet
sprinkled in the E-region
of ionosphere. Nice hit.

We cannot stand it
or stand idly by.
It is a test of strength.

Teresa in her kitchen
baking nut rolls and bread,
an instant ago sang a folksong
sweetly out of key.
Weld her flesh to the stove
and to bedrock. Well done.

Otherwise we are nothing.
People would walk on our backs,
we couldn't speak
or raise our eyes
or go outside off a chain leash.

Dmitri in his crib,
eight weeks old,
learns to use his eyes
and gurgles.
Bring his internal organs
to a rapid boil.
Simmer them midair
out of his skin.

All the earth contaminant,
Christ and Marx done proud.

Big brave athletically accomplished men
with clear minds and in a time of peace
figured this out and decided it was best.

Tom Hawkins

HERITAGE

I. Endangered Species

The Consolidated-Vultee B-36 'Condor',
nine bomb-bays, four turrets,
range 8,000 miles, could drop to death
twenty-one tons from forty thousand.
Phased out in '58, it never saw combat.

II. Drop-Shot

Europe would fall in ten short days.
Britain holding out through forty nuclear hits.
Suffering eighty percent losses,
air-crews would mutiny. Half America might die.
Yet war would remain war
as mankind has always known it. We would win.

This plan was scrapped with 230-foot wingspans,
ten engines, three pilots, three gunners,
two navigators, & two anesthetized bombardiers.

III. Detente

Consolidated-Vultee became Convair,
dinosaur-birds yielding to the B-58A 'Hustler'.
It hit Mach 2.1 in level flight,
the fastest Western bomber ever deployed,
yet with a three-man crew & 55-ton load,
was obsolete by 1960.

Abandoned on Mojave sand and mud,
squadrons point like silver arrows
alternately toward Los Angeles & Las Vegas.

Merritt Clifton

R.I.P.

Four minutes from launching,
submarine-fired cruise missiles
could strike the heart of the country.

Ashes to ashes, dust to dust returneth.

We can rest assured, says the Pentagon,
that all possible has been done
to insure continuity of government.

Merritt Clifton

SONG OF THE CENTURY

Sing of moon journeys and artificial satellites,
Ideas and impulses transmitted across air and space,
People and matter transported faster than sound's speed,
Robot calculation, storage, organization of data
In quantum manner beyond comprehension,
Disease rampant millenia conquered,
More mankind better fed and sheltered with
Greater dignity and freedom than
Since the dawn of time.

Sing of twenty millions
Slaughtered in the Great War
    on the beaches of Gallipoli,
    on the fields of Flanders,
Of the massacred
    in the Warsaw Ghetto,
    in the Katyn Forest,
    in front of the Tsar's palace,
    at Wounded Knee,
Of the genocide
    against the starving Armenians,
    against the landed Kulaks,
    against the wandering Rom,
    against the children of Israel,
    against the tribes of Brazil,
Of the sanctioned brutality
    by the OGPU, NKVD, AVO, SS, GeStaPo,
    by the Greek, Chilean and Turkish officers
    by the North Korean brainwashers.

Sing of the South Vietnamese tiger cages,
    of the British internment camps,
    of the American Indian reservations,
    of the Japanese-American internment camps,
    of the Japanese prisoner of war camps,
    of the French and British penal colonies,
        of Andersonville, of Auschwitz,
        of Devil's Island, of Dachau.

Sing of the dive bombs of Guernica,
    of the blitz bombs of London,
    of the fire bombs of Hamburg,
    of the ultimate bombs
        of Hiroshima,
        of Nagasaki.

A. Swanson

Frank Higgins

THE 69TH REGIMENT

When the first World War began I was of draft age, but I was already married and we had our first child. Three of my cousins were drafted. I visited them in their training camps several times, especially one of my cousins who took me to his camp several times and showed me how he was trained for combat. When he would demonstrate how he was drilled to me he told me that he was practicing how to get the best results with his bayonet. He knew he had to strike the enemy between the ribs so that the bayonet wouldn't be deflected by the ribs on its way to the enemies heart. He also showed me many other ways to kill the enemy.

My cousin, although a strong, well developed young man, had seldom been in a fist fight let alone actually combat, but he wrote to me from France that he was now in the trenches on the battlefield, ready to strike the enemy although he didn't know who the enemy was. My point is—he didn't come back. The other two cousins were not combat quality so they were performing other duties which didn't cost them their lives and they came back.

As the war progressed, the army started to draft fathers of one child and I was registered for the draft. Although I was a devoted patriot and loved my country I was not ready to give my life for my country. I was convinced that none of those corpses buried in those beautifully trimmed cemeterys in France who had given their lives for their country even knew why their lives were taken from them without their consent.

Anyway, I prayed to God that I would be spared and my prayers were answered. My wife gave birth of our second son and my prayers and my wife kept me from being drafted.

Before being sent to France, the recruits had parades in which they marched the length of New York City toward the south ferry where the ships which carried them overseas were docked. I, as many others, enjoyed those parades passing before our eyes, and one of the parades impressed me as no other, even to this stage of my life I still see it in my memories. It was a regiment called the "Fighting 69th." Those men were all six footers, Irishmen, and the pride of the army. All of those infantry soldiers marched holding their guns with the butts in the right hand the barrels on their shoulders, but the 69th carried their guns with both hands in a position ready to strike the enemy with the bayonet.

Girls on both sides of the streets were throwing flowers on them. The ground was shaking under their feet when they passed before me. Sadly enough, the 69th regiment which was the pride of the army, were thrown immediately into combat in France and as soon as they reached the battlefield 80% of them fell before the enemy, but they will live in our hearts forever.

Rubin Zar

TOMBSTONES

When we bake bread we use an oven and flour,
When we build a house we use building material and a level.
In war we use ammunition and manpower
Dominated by our military, inspired by the devil.

Because some generals may become great
Soldiers join the ranks of the late
Compelled by leaders in their so-called strife
The young are shamefully robbed of their life.

The dead bodies were our enemies
The fallen soldiers were our friends
The dead bodies went to kill
The fallen soldiers went to defend.
They assaulted each other with no soulful ill feelings
Only dominance spurred on that killing.

Now they are laid at rest
Each departed from his dearest
Robbed of their life and love
With tombstones as their nearest.

Have you ever heard a Mother's lament,
When they take away her only son
Who unwillingly is sent
His young life to disown.
Many differ from cannibals only in name
Many of our triumphant killers
Can be found in the hall of fame.

Rubin Zar

ANDERSONVILLE SOUVENIR THUMB SCREWS

We say we could sell these folks Brooklyn Bridge,
or a piece of the true Cross if we lived
where blood clogged the chariot wheels,
where bishops' books resolved the world;
but people who 'buy' Brooklyn Bridge invest,
aren't drawn to Dachau in droves
or Andersonville by the carload
to wander around the grounds.

We sell souvenir grey caps, souvenir blue;
mostly, we sell souvenir thumb screws
to the people
who take pictures of themselves locked in cells,
who shake their heads at shackles in the wall,
who look as long at the hot box or latrine
as crowds in the Capitol watch the Constitution.

Even now, North in Gettysburg,
they board tour buses that bray Pickett's charge,
clamber over rocks on Little Round Top;
and off among the apple trees
they look for slugs in tree trunks;
photograph old barns with shrapnel scars,
Lincoln's pledge on a brass plaque.

Frank Higgins

July 4, 1976
Eldon City Park, Eldon, Missouri
(Frank Higgins)

from THE NATIVES CRY

I remember the hunt.
Many buffalo killed for the people.
No famine, no cold in the winter;
But I was young then.
Before the white man came,
With his Iron Horse and civilization.
Life has changed.
No longer free   to roam the plains,
No longer free to hunt,
Many were killed, but too late.
Peace we offered,
Trust we gave,
Now all have turned on us.
Red savages we were called,
By those who slaughtered our families.
There will be no buffalo this winter,
Only the sound of wailing
By those left to live in civilization.

Kate Corwin

STORY FROM A MOUNTAIN

Palm trees,
long and slender swaying palm trees:
Like brownfinned Mermaids
of earth
green eyes
danced in the sunsetting breeze
moist
with this ancient sea
that enfolds us
spilling its oceanfloor jewels
wet
into the cup of our nets;
And this,
like the waves that come
to tumble
soft
on our sand

drew the ships to our shores
and the horses
And armored men
And the chains!

Christian soldiers,
they called themselves
Gods
with flags & guns
in helmets of steel
they came
with their swords drawn
against our offering of dancers;
Earth Beans
flying in the night
flying through fire & stars
smokelessly

The fruits,
soft in their rainbowcolor
so like the laughter that once came
to children
unaware
the war
were crushed beneath the weight
of marchingboots
And the swords,
so much the god of thunder
fell heavy
on our homes
hugged into final mothersmiles
the children
were murdered

Caoyuca
Ponce
Sierra Maestra
Algiers

Pass your hand,
tender
this body that bleeds;
Mylai
And this swollen eye
that is Wounded Knee.

Jesus Papoleto Melendez

THE VIETNAM LEGACY

The American Friends Service Committee recently sent an inquiry to the Vietnamese medical staff of a physical rehabilitation center in central South VietNam. The Committee wanted to know how they could assist this facility, which they had founded under the name of The Quakers Prosthetic Center during the war years, in Quang Ngai, and which has since been relocated to the more central city of Qui Nhon.

The reply they received included an inventory of needed supplies, some of which are listed below:

Prosthetic Supplies
Crutch Tips
Crutch Armpit Cushions
Stump Sox

Limb Parts and Accesories
Below-the-Knee Joint
Alumininum Ankle Joint Extensions
Knee Joint Brace
Aluminum Short Leg Brace
Hip Joint
Above-the-Elbow Parts
Below-the-Elbow Parts
Arm Joints

Additional Categories
Pneumatic Stump Shrinker
Ankle Joint Feet
Cosmetic Movable Hand
Pelvic Joint

Occupational therapy
Braille Typewriter
Hearing Aids
Long Canes for the Blind

It does not take great insight to recognize that in an age of numbered credit cards, bank accounts and driver's licenses, of nightly news reports on traffic fatalities, crime in the streets and natural disasters, Americans find it difficult to see individual human beings among the casualties of Viet-Nam:

Vietnamese killed, wounded or made refugees	13,457,822
Orphans and half-orphans	879,745
Amputees (by 1973)	88,260
Americans killed	55,869

But there is no such comprehension problem with the list the Quakers received. How can we not respond?

I am not ashamed to say I weep at Mark Jury's photo of a triple-amputee Vietnamese child named Dao, struggling alone through her tears to manage cumbersome aluminum braces and three ''prosthetic devices.''

Rather, I am reminded of philosopher Jean-Paul Satre's admonition to his people (during the French war in Algeria): ''It is not right, my fellow-countrymen, you who know very well all the crimes committed in our name, it's not at all right that you do not breathe a word about them to anyone, not even your own soul, for fear of having to stand in judgement of yourself.''

There is nothing, now, that can be done about ''our involvement in Viet-Nam,'' or the fruitless debate over whether or not there were crimes. There are, indeed, wounds, as the above medical list so graphically reminds us.

What is the response to a request for ''Above-the-Elbow Arm Parts'' or a ''Cosmetic Movable Hand''? And how long dare we wait to respond? Is not our very humanity, to say nothing of America's destiny, here at stake? Did not the years of ''Vietnam'' forever interlock the healing of our wounds—believe me, they are profound—to those of the people of Viet-Nam?

There is no issue or problem before us, from energy to unemployment, that is unrelated to ''the era of Vietnam.'' Nor will any amount of Congressional debate or Presidential committees be able to turn the tide until we decide on an overall healing process. Until we return to the root.

What if our President, who uttered a healing resolve, started the process himself, one so broad in scope it encompassed every conceivable relevant problem? The reuniting of refugee families, here and in Viet-Nam. The ''boat people.'' Our own discarded and anguished veterans. Objectors who sought refuge abroad. Tons of unexploded ordnance still, to this day, in the ground. And the pitiful cries of children like Dao which echo down the tunnels of our consciences.

Do we ask so much, my fellow-Americans, for a leadership with vision? How can the most momentous crises of our lives be solved by piecemeal and often faltering solutions? There must be a thread which binds it all together, which gives us a reason for carrying on.

And in the meantime, we as individuals need not be told what it is that we have to do. We can start, one by one, to help those who suffer, here and in Viet-Nam.

Richard Hughes

JUNGLE SHIRT BOOGIE ON A CONCRETE PLAIN

fast steppin'
side street walkin'
away from the
            noise
and insanity

side street thinkin'
drill sergeant's hat down
low
shades the
            eyes
jungle boots
            rocking
with the movement
            of my feet
stayin' cool inside
jungle shirt
many pockets
o.d. green

side street trippin'
people staring
yet avoiding
            my eyes
what the hell is that?
            (their eyes scream)

I live on top of
            a mountain
            (my thoughts reply)
can't you tell?
with sheath knife
and honing stone
montagnard bracelet and
jungle fatigues

watchin' the buzzard's
           flight
or laying on the
cool
green
earth
with many thousand
           flowers
can you?

Or
standing
facing
the raging wind
jungle shirt tails
           flying

have you ever gone out
           and hugged
the fog
           as it drifted
past your home
have you?
           down here
           in this
insanity?

these are
           my thoughts
while I

jungle shirt boogie
on a
           concrete
           plain.

Steve Hassna

HAVE YOU FELT?

I have felt it a thousand times
I have seen it much too often
       Have you?
The U.S. comes to you with their smiles
       and their lies
And say "Serve!"
They come to you with their rank
       and their flag
And say "Be Proud!"
Then they come to you
And say "Die!"
And when they touch you it is cold
It is damp and it is clammy
       Why is this? you ask
It shouldn't be this way to serve.
But to serve is to kill,
So it's cold.
       Why should it be death?
Because death is your service
And it's damp.
       Then why are you proud?
Because to serve is pride.
But to serve is to die
So it's clammy.

Steven Hassna

MEMORIES OF TOMORROW

       All men my brothers
All women, my kin
For the unborn babies
    I dream
Pushing and struggling, kicking
       and screaming
So goes life's story
So goes my dream
       Hard times and sorrow
       clutch at my soul
       Memories of tomorrow
       all that I know.

Steven Hassna

HOW I WILL KNOW WHEN THE WAR IS OVER

we are all assigned wars
we are all assigned friends who die
in war during years of private war
we are assigned men to love who burn
draft cards go to prison
we are all assigned men to love who conscientiously object
to everything
but peace

i thought my war was over
all my patient marching
my strong left hand writing slogans on flags
to carry on my strong left shoulder

i thought my war was over
when my friend with one leg blown away
in war blew his brains out carefully in his garage
his strong right hand holding the gun

i thought my war was over
when i stopped writing poems
about nixon and god and babies burning

i was wrong
today all this week all last week
the war comes back
i was wrong because my son says
"today i met a man who writes about vietnam.
was that your war, mom?"
i was wrong because my son says
"here's a picture in the paper of the man.
does he say words about war in his story?"
i answer and realize
my son wants to share my war until he gets one
of his own

we are all assigned children to love
they may not come from our bodies that hardly matters
but we all must claim children to love
we are all assigned children to learn from
to teach the wearying truths of war to

we are all assigned a war and i have mine
i must not forget
there is always one more poem to write
and i must not forget
that the title of this poem is a lie
there will never be any way for me to know
that the war is over

Deborah Keenan

A MESSAGE IN COURT NO. 4

To have a childhood colored with the memories of a brother
Younger, spirited like myself...but different;
energetic like myself...but different.
So many similiarities...so many differences.
Our lives blended and contrasted
like the hues of a masterful painting
until the night I did not hear his name.

In a bunk...in a barracks...in Texas.
I listened and did not hear his name.
He was missing...missing in Korea.
To hear his name would mean he lived...
I did not hear his name.

It has been many years since that night and life has been good;
I have thought of him often...and yet, not enough.
There have been more wars...more fear;
the nations of the world have not yet learned to live together.

Recently, my brother and I met again...
In a cemetary in Hawaii.
On a sunny afternoon, I stood in front of a wall...
His name was there...and so...his memory.

In court No. 4, in the ''courts of the missing'' we met...
or seemed to meet. The memories...my life...his death...
peace...and something else was there in Court No. 4...
''war''...the smell of it...the uncertainty of it...
the injustice of it...and most of all...
the result of it.

There seemed to be a message there...
in Court No. 4...a message about war.
The message was not precise...
I could not see or hear it clearly...
Perhaps it was not for me...
Perhaps it was for someone else...
Perhaps it is for some leader who
wishes to have his people go to war...
or some politician who espouses war as a solution...
to those or *anyone* who is so inclined...
Go...
Go on a sunny afternoon and face the wall...
Look high up...near the top...you'll see his name.
John J. Dzienis...
Go and talk to him in Court No. 4
Discuss with him...
Your war.

Don Dzienis

234

from TWENTY YEARS AFTER

1.

In l977, as they/we stockpile neutron bombs
which destroy only life, not property
children stroll slowly home from school
through radioactive rain
carrying mutated, defective genes
clutching schoolbooks celebrating war
yearning for uniforms and guns
holding already congealed concepts
of we and they--properly socialized
made too stupid to love.
As Dr. Schweitzer said in 1957
"the awareness that we are all human beings together
has been lost in war and through politics."

2.

In this time of fatal irreverence for life
with little heart or time to read
why does this woman, this Jew,
read what a Christian man wrote
years ago in isolated Lambarene?
My shelves nag with the latest works
of seasoned conflict resolution theorists
and new disarmament proposers, peace resolvers
all hiding the blood in comforting complexity.
Deterrence has gone wild and foolishness reigns.
I re-read Schweitzer's comment — a prophecy —
"the newest scientific knowledge may be allied
with an entirely unreflecting view of the universe."

3.

Between the wars
they mourn the dead
and hide the wounded
and speak of peace
meanwhile arming.

4.

I do not study Schweitzer because he said
women have special responsibility to seek peace
though, as a mother, I acknowledge this.
I return to him because in a mad world
his words cut as surely through sham
as his surgeon's scalpel excised pathology.
Twenty years ago, he reminded us
"the spirit is a mighty force for transforming things."
We shall have peace, only if we wish it enough
as he said, to "rediscover the fact that
we all together are human beings."

5.

As a sociologist, I know how difficult it is
to break the gun-casing put on our humanity.
Society gives wrong messages to children
and wrong orders and rewards to adults.
Everyone learns about the generals;
my new students have forgotten Schweitzer
or only know he founded a hospital.

6.

Some of us were awakened
during World War II.
As a young reporter, I walked daily
through trains of three-tiered stretchers
with mutilated men, my age then,
glad to leave the killing
but never young again.
I also walked through trains of caskets.
I walk there still.
The fellowship of those who bear
the mark of pain needs members.
My students must go to the veterans' hospital:
Vicarious pain is better than none.
Yet even the wounded forget
and offer up their sons.

7.

During Viet Nam, I too protested
incredulous as they/we ate dinner
looking at videotapes of burning villages,
burning flesh.
Later my student-veterans
wept to me their despair and guilt.
The monsters were our children.
Where is their comfort and ours?

8.

The policy makers tell us international relations
are so complex
it is even hard to remember the names
that separate us into nationhood.
I have sat through their lectures
and know all the formulas.
Read my students' notes:
"War is the residual social institution
for settling otherwise insoluable conflict.
Until a better institution is developed,
we will continue to have war.
Developing a better institution is unlikely
as long as we lack what Dr. Schweitzer called
"A feeling of mutual trustworthiness toward each other."

Putting it another way,
as did sociologist George Herbert Mead,
until we can take the role of the other
no matter where he lives or what his pigmentation
we shall continue to define certain others
as killable non-humans.

10.

This year, as sabbatical, I attend medical school.
At 52, for the first time,
glimpse wonders of the cell and human body
so marvelous and beautiful that even good physicians
aren't really sure how it all works.
But a bullet can stop life instantly,
Lungs are a marvel of design
but fallout destroys a million lungs.
Now I understand Schweitzer's passion.
I no longer kill insects.

11.

Schweitzer didn't like Africans hearing of European wars,
He was ashamed of models offered.
Perhaps we need shame before our children.
We could get the animal cages out of schools
and replace the flag on Iwo Jima photo
with Kaethe Kollowitz's war portraits.
We cannot let them be deceived again.

12.

I read Schweitzer because I teach.
It is hard to find words and symbols
in a time of crying for better ones
then we give our youth.
One despairs if one cannot remember
what a man can do and be
if he has morality and will.
Schweitzer teaches us this.
As he said, ''at times our own light goes out
and is rekindled by a spark from another person.''
We need his reverence for life *now*
when technology multiplies inhumanity
destructiveness is so commonplace
we do not really notice
that our children walk in radioactive rain
preparing for another war.

Ruth Harriet Jacobs

JUNE 20, 1977. LAST YEAR, THIS YEAR

1
Along Thirty-fourth Street in New York.
in the wide, dove-shadowed street,
a procession.
First a streamer that says
        BOSTON TO WASHINGTON
        WALK FOR DISARMAMENT
                &
        SOCIAL JUSTICE
Jim Peck has one end, I the other.
Behind us a group of Japanese
skull-shaven monks and nuns
in saffron or rust-colored robes
classically rippling at their strong
ankles and in their hands
fan drums. Mamoru Kato

meditative in his drum-protected quiet.
Beside him, Masotochi Shibuya
with his thin form, a patient organizer.
Then Hideo Morioka, a sane saint,
and Yoshiko Miyana, a poet (not a nun),
her heavy black hair falling
on her forehead. Others as well,
all walking
with the long line of Americans
eastward to the United Nations.
Their chant is a prolonged cymbal,
''Namu myo ho ren ge kyo,''
the ''kyo'' little more than ''ko,''
repetitive syllables with their drum
accompaniment. The fan drum is a disk
of reverberent stretched membrane like a fan
held in the left hand,
the stick in the right hand
hitting hard. After every fifth beat,
a ruffle. On and on.
        ''The people of Hiroshima
ask nothing of the world...''*

2
Last year, in both New York and Washington,
I walked with these monks and nuns and Yoshiko.
They were from the Japan Buddha Sangha.
In all, sixteen Japanese
were in the American
Continental Walk for Disarmament
and Social Justice. Some walked
from San Francisco to Washington,
some on ''feeder walks''
from New Orleans, Boston, other cities, coming
from the A-bombed country to be
here with us for peace.

3
This year
in memory/recognition of that
companionship sealed
in eight thousand miles of walking here,
the Sangha is asking Americans
to come and be their guests
in the Japanese annual Peace March
from Tokyo to Hiroshima.
              I read the invitation
in the War Resisters League bulletin
and phoned Jim Peck.
As I half expected, he told me
he was going. I told him
I was much tempted to go.
He said, ''I hope you do.''

Millen Brand

*''The people of Hiroshima ask nothing of the world except that
we be allowed to offer ourselves as an exhibit for peace. We ask
only that enough people know what happened here and how it
happened and why it happened, and that they work hard to see
that it never happens again.''
              Shinzo Hamai, Mayor of Hiroshima, 1949

JULY 7. ON THE AFTERNOON MARCH

After climbing a long hill,
we have a rest period and sit beside the road.
I sit by the Vice President
of the All Japan Day-Pay Workers Union local,
an older man like me. We are silent
behind our separate languages, though
the glance between us is friendly.
There is no interpreter with us.
The VP rubs his legs, kneading
his tired muscles. I start to knead mine too,
and he shows me on his own legs:
Do it this way, get
the muscles relaxed.
He offers me a cigarette. I shake my head no.
He imitates smoking and shakes his head, meaning,
You don't smoke. I nod that he is right.
I point to the sun. A gesture of his says,
Yes, it is hot.
When we resume marching,
he gets up first, reaches his hand to me,
and pulls me up. Again
a look between us, of friends.
We know we have had a
good conversation.

Millen Brand

240

JULY 14. THE MARCHERS

This afternoon
lined against a wall waiting to start,
five old women with moles, wens,
tight knots of hair, and ordinary dresses
falling straight down to ordinary
legs. Near them several working women and men
with calf-length cotton trousers
and white cloths, under their hats,
covering the backs of their necks, the sexes
like a reflection of each other.
Since marchers go only one day,
many can take off from work.
Teachers walk with us,
waving to students on the roadside
and the students wave back.
Children run along with us.
     In America the walkers were special--
movement people, the dedicated.
Here they are just people.
Captain Shigetoshi tells me,
''Wave--it's good to wave.''
Many pause on village streets
as we go by, interrupt talk or shopping,
and wave. A dance of arms back and forth.
An old woman with a baby waves.
A universal
sympathy, a unity.
A hand that presses
a stray hair behind the ear
holds a banner, a man who walks the street
in a blue kimono bows.
The people walk, the people watch.

Millen Brand

JULY 21. A FAMILY FOR PEACE

Miss Ishida says,
"My whole family works for peace.
My parents and my brother Yasutaka.
They belong to the local peace committee.
My brother works for the small-scale
industrial workers union
and works too for the poor,
for people with heavy taxes.
He and his wife
help them calculate their tax,
so they will know what to pay."
        At a meeting at Onga
I meet Miss Ishida's mother and father.
Her father is on the city council
and gives a speech of greeting. Afterward
I come up to him to shake his hand.
I put out my hand. He does not move.
His wife says, "*Amerikano*,"
and tells him I want to shake his hand. Quickly
he puts out his hand and I take it.
        He is blind.

Millen Brand

JULY 23. MOJI STATION

At noon and still in Kitakyushu,
half a hundred new marchers
meet us at Moji Station.
Among them is a man
with white hair, thin and fine,
down the back of his neck. Yet
he looks young. He takes my hand.
His name is Yojiro Taya.
I tell him I am seventy-one.
He says he is seventy-six
and again takes my hand.
"Haiku," he says. He explains
through our interpreter,
"For fifty-five years
I have been walking around Japan
Writing haiku."
     "What kind?" I ask him.
     "All kinds. Country scenes,
nature, the seasons, but mainly
in the last twenty years
haiku against war."
     "And now you're marching with us."
     "Every year I've marched
in demonstrations against war.
I march and write.
I've written thousands of haiku." Seventeen syllables,
each a breath
against death.

Millen Brand

AUGUST 2. THE MUSEUM

Jim and I walk down from the temple
to the Peace Museum. Its single floor,
unlike Nagasaki's
Atomic Bomb Material Center,
is carefully planned. A central pit
with a model of Hiroshima
after the bomb. Devastation
clear to the mountains. Everywhere except where
a low hill saved some houses.
Photographs of the leveled areas.
A life-size model of three victims
walking half-naked, reddened, with skin dripping
from their fingers. The expression
staring, stunned, a look of nonunderstanding,
a look saying,
"We do not know what it is."
Stone crumbled, wall copings raised
far from the hypocenter, women, girls
losing the pride of their hair, their heads
bowed. Burned tongues, burned jaws.
Eyes ruined, and as in Nagasaki
clocks stopped, here with the hands
at eight fifteen. The moment
when every ordinary motion
of work, of walking, raising a cup to the lips
ended.
    Near the exit a sign says in English,
"So that was how Hiroshima perished."

Millen Brand

TO LEARN FROM HIROSHIMA

Hiroshima Peace Park is a very beautiful place, especially during the Cherry Blossom Season in April. One can relax, look at the trees reflected in the canals, and almost forget that this was the site of the largest instantaneous mass killing in history. A shattered building with a skeleton dome reminds us. So do several monuments with names and the date, August 7, 1945, inscribed in Japanese.

There was a time when I would argue that nuclear bombs should not have been dropped on Hiroshima or Nagasaki. My standard rebuttals were usually effective against the standard nauseums about it being necessary to end the war and save lives. A visit to the Memorial Museum, in the center of the park, can destroy such an academic approach. For the people of the sister ''Peace Cities,'' as they are called, the debate has little meaning. They experienced the Bomb, and those who remained afterwards do not see their psychic and physical scars in terms of an intellectual exercise.

The museum is not there to denounce the attack, nor is it a ''war crimes exhibit.'' It was built because the survivors felt the rest of the world should know about nuclear weapons. Displays and documentary photographs serve the purpose well. A scale model shows what the city looked like immediately after the explosion. Life-size statues in a glass case show what those who lived through it looked like. Technical information is given on the effects at different distances from the epicenter. . . .a percentage died instantly here, a percentage of the wounded survived there; some were blinded here, and some were burned there; and this many died a few hours later from the following injuries. . . It all runs together after a while, the figures reaching into the hundred thousands.

The blast heat intensity caused color-altering chemical changes in the surfaces of granite blocks—except where people happened to be standing or sitting at the time. Their disintegrating bodies sheltered the rock long enough to leave permanent ''shadows'' as silent memorials to unknown victims. During reconstruction suffering continued in the form of attacks from a mystery ''atom bomb disease.'' Symptoms were (and still are) cancer, leukemia, keloids, and several strange disorders. Punishment extends to the yet unborn, for many now carry genetic defects in their blood lines. Deformed and retarded children, born every year, cry out to us that the nuclear bomb did not end the war, nor did it bring peace.

The rest of the walk through the park was a time to contemplate what I had just seen. Visitors were affected differently. An American matron sobbed. A South African couple wrote, "Nothing happens without God's will," in the guest book.

Although the majority of Americans were respectful and compassionate, a few were offended by what was displayed and missed the point entirely. They wrote, "You guys seem to have forgotten about Pearl Harbor," and "Japan started it." Someone from Texas said, "Better here than in the U.S."

I controlled myself and tried to sort out some flashbacks to a time when I learned a little about nuclear warfare. It was in Annapolis, at the United States Naval Academy, during the summer of 1971, between my sophomore and junior years as a midshipman. A series of week-long programs was designed to acquaint us with various career specialties we could enter after graduation. As one of a few Far Eastern Relations majors, I was already quite alienated by the war in Southeast Asia, and the week of lectures on submarines did not improve my attitude.

The "indoctrination" (their word for it) was an impressive affair—all very secret we were told, and no notes could be taken. Some officers discussed the training programs we would take if we chose "nukes." Others talked about the extra pay we would get. One said he'd extended his commitment three years for a $15,000 cash bonus. He was honest enough to admit that money was the only reason he remained in the Navy.

Some spoke about global strategy and how they were responsible for maintaining world peace. A few went on about technical details. . . .this missile has a range of so many thousand miles and this one has seven warheads. This submarine carries sixteen inter-continental ballistic missiles but our next one will have twenty-four. The effective area of destruction for these bombs has a diameter of. . . Here too, the figures ran together like a crazed nightmare, adding up to the scorching of the earth several times over. For good measure there were submarines that would survive total war and still have weapons to launch in case any enemies lingered in the rubble.

Maps, and diagrams, and graphs, and more details made it all very clear. . . .here is a missile which is very accurate and has a warhead equivalent in strength to three times the Hiroshima Bomb. Now this other one carries a warhead twenty times as powerful. It's not as accurate, as you can see from the graph, but as you can see from the size of the circular area of destruction on the chart, it doesn't have to be. . . The audience of young midshipmen found this very funny for some reason and all but a few laughed. Such was their level of consciousness at that time. Some of them now serve aboard nuclear submarines.

Many questions were asked, not all of which were answered. Most were. "Sir, do we target civilian as well as military areas in the Soviet Union?"

"Well, you can't hit the shipyards in Murmansk without hitting the people in Murmansk," came the reply.

"Sir, do you know the names of your targets?" one commander was asked.

"I have the co-ordinates. I could look them up in an atlas if I wanted to, I guess, but it's only academic to me."

Perhaps he hadn't seen enough of the world, or enjoyed the beauty of life enough to know that no place on the globe is a set of co-ordinates. And if he ever visits Hiroshima, maybe he will understand that destroyed humanity is not an academic issue.

New and better weapons have been developed since those lectures, and more are on the drawing boards. The inventory is a litany of man's capacity of perversion. . . .anti-personnel bombs with fragments that cannot be X-rayed; CBU-72 explosive devices which "ruptured the intestines of sheep hidden in trenches," according to the gleeful announcements of Honeywell testers; secret electronic gadgets read about only in the wildest science fiction; dolphins trained to participate in various sorts of underwater warfare; and $250,000 invested in testing the Frisbee for possible combat use. . . In the future, if not already with us, are laser beam warfare, satellite warfare, and weather warfare. The imagination of the doomsday planners never ends. Totally new concepts in ship propulsion and hull design will revolutionize naval strategy. In 1971, when the established order still wasn't quite sure what it was going to do about Vietnam or the energy crisis, it could comfortably discuss the speed of aircraft carriers in the year 2000.

It is thus with a sense of rage that I read reports about the United States "falling behind" in face of the "growing Soviet military threat." Invariably call are made for greater preparedness and increased spending on armaments. The evidence and logic presented are usually so overwhelming that "liberal" politicians are regularly co-opted into supporting the hawkish demands of the war industry.

Progressive thinkers and activist would be mistaken in belittling or denying the existence of a Soviet buildup. Their growing fleets and facilities overseas are no mirage. We might argue that Russian paranoia is justified by their having suffered dreadfully from three foreign invasions in this century, and by the great network of American bases around the world. Nonetheless, it is evident that the best instincts of their revolution have long since worn thin. . . .

What should be understood as the essence of the Superpower confrontation is that the militarists of both parties have a simbiotic relationship and belong to the framework of one structure. With each justifying its own parasitic existence, the two continually provide each other with excuses for further growth. Always pointing to some threatening new development in the opposite partner they manage to swindle their respective societies out of more talent and resources. Both use each other, need each other and want each other.

The rise of Admiral Gorshkov in the Soviet Union was closely related to American actions during the Cuban Missile Crisis. For years he had been kept in the background by the Kremlin and his requests for ocean-going fleets were for the most part disregarded. The dramatic confrontation between U.S. Navy destroyers and Russian freighters loaded with missiles altered the situation completely. As the blockaded ships headed back to the Soviet Union Gorshkov was listened to and given a free hand in expanding his navy. Never again would they suffer humiliation from lack of naval power. The process of developing weapons systems as complex as modern cruisers and destroyers can take over a dozen years from initial planning to final launching. Hence the "sudden" buildup in this field can be seen as a response to the challenge met by the Soviet Navy in October of 1962.

American officers love Gorshkov. Having in effect promoted him to power, they can now point to his ships as proof that they need more of the same. His book, *Red Star Rising At Sea*, was even published in the United States by the U.S. Naval Institute and serialized in its professional journal, *The Proceedings*. It reads much like a similar book, *The Influence of Sea Power Upon History*, by Alfred T. Mahan, a nineteenth century American imperialist, who also advocated a strong ocean-going navy. . .

*   *   *

A further contribution to the dynamics of arms races lies in the nature of the military career. A young pilot just out of flight school wants to fly the newest aircraft and no sailor wants to chip paint on an old rustbucket. This causes a flow of pressure energy from the bottom up for more money, more equipment, and more toys. The process becomes acute higher in the ranks. For a U.S. Navy commander to be promoted to captain, he usually has to serve a "command at sea" tour. There are more commanders than there are billets available. Hence the more ships that can be hustled out of Congress, the greater the chances for a command and subsequent promotion. Few would risk their careers by testifying that a particular weapon was useless or unneeded. Such a tendency, backed by public relations budgets and bribing powers of armaments industries, is a strong force to reckon with.

A major controversy within the Navy concerned the *Spruance* class destroyer. Some exceptional officers presented evidence, and an article was even published in *The Proceedings*, condemning it as having dubious military value. Still, those who had careers vested in the fate of the *Spruance* were more numerous and Litton Industries had its cronies on Capitol Hill. Today we are blessed with more than twenty of the contraptions. Four had been pawned off to the [then] Shah of Iran. Doubtless this situation with variations exists in the Soviet Union and in any other country that buys or manufactures military hardware.

*   *   *

The mechanics of the Superpower military rivalry are not overly complex. The wasteful needs of the warrior classes in both empires are served by the best talent, labor, and resources of their respective societies. The masses of each have no real quarrel with each other except through illusions created by history and maintained by their present warlords. The majority are propagandized into believing that their sacrifices are necessary for protection foreign threats. Learning only the negative aspects of their "enemies," they prepare for the worst, and ultimately bring out the worst potential in each other.

A few statesmen claim to have seen through the process and do their best to halt it through such activities as the Strategic Arms Limitation Talks. They triumphantly return announcing "ceilings" of 2,400 major implements of Hiroshima death. Negotiators of this ilk cannot be taken seriously, must less trusted. They quibble about whether a particular missile or bomber should be labeled "strategic" or "tactical" as though it would matter to the victims. When negotiations stall they give the go-ahead for more weapons deployment and refer to it as gaining more "bargaining chips."

Any arms-control treaty actually signed would be immediately scrutinized for loopholes. Agreements made at the Washington Conference of 1921-22 limited the sizes of signatories' fleets according to the numbers of ships and total tonnages. Naval architecture and industry worldwide took a leap forward as shipbuilders designed new vessels that would carry more guns per ton afloat. We should not expect more of modern treaty makers from any nation. They invariably lack the spirit necessary for true accomodation.

Change will come only if societies reject the suicidal cycle *en masse*. Much as the strengthening of one military force leads to the buildup of its rival, so the reduction of one should lead to the withering of the other. A victory for sanity in America would be a boost for more creative interests in the Soviet Union.

How do we answer those good citizens who fear that such a process will not take place? What if "they" continue to expand as "we" withdraw? There should be no concern that Russian soldiers and sailors enjoy their duties any more than their American counterparts do. When our soldiers are out of western Europe, the Red Army officers will have no excuses to give their men for being in eastern Europe. When no American ships are in the Mediterranean the Soviets will have a hard time justifying a presence there.

Good reason exists to believe that the Red Army is already having difficulties with men who are tired of war games. The defection of Belenko, a MIG-25 pilot from the most trusted ranks of the officer corps, is one sign. About two years ago a group of Russian sailors mutinied and had a destroyer well on its way to Sweden before it was crippled by air attacks. That enough men were able to cooperate in their rebellion to get a ship out of harbor shows that military dissent may be much higher than in the United States.

As Americans our duty lies in the launching of a people's moral equivalent to war (the expression is not Carter's) against the Armed Forces. Everything from overseas troop withdrawals and budget cutbacks by Congress to strikes on the part of soldiers should be considered positive developments. Men and women in uniform everywhere must be asked to search their consciences. Workers in war profiteering industries should be educated about their roles. Wherever we are we must encourage people not to enlist—teachers their students, parents their children, students their classmates. The offensive against R.O.T.C. on campuses should be renewed. Military recruiters are invading high schools and seducing naive teenagers. They should be confronted. The counter-recruitment program of the Central Committee for Conscientious Objectors is a noble effort in this direction.

No other issue is as serious as the militarist threat which faces humanity today. Certainly it is important to be concerned with economic injustices, ecological problems, overpopulation and starvation, and various liberation movements around the world. We all have our private Palestines to be passionate about. But we will have none of these if the armed madness is allowed to play itself out to its ultimate conclusion.

The warships will stay in port when there are too few sailors to man them and the guns will rust when soldiers refuse to carry them. The battlefield pawns must reach out to each other across their trenches in spite of their leaders. Our responsibility to Life is to encourage them in this direction. If we succeed, we will save the earth from the fate of a final Hiroshima.

William G. Kelsey

I saw the death machines,
grim, fierce, gray.
We praise our country's peace
but still
we build the death machines.

In our slavery,
we march to work
to build the death machines
and we sink
to their protection.

Entombed in steel,
there are men
beneath the sea,
riding the death machines.

Shackled above,
we victims
rejoice, for
our children can eat —
until the death machines
point to us.

Shel Horowitz

DEATH DEALERS

"We are the hollow men;
we are the stuffed men."

Except for the armed guards,
it could be an auto show.
Except for the uniforms,
it could be a street fair.

But it's nothing so harmless;
these are clean-handed killers,
with their guns, copters, missiles.
They'll never be tried for murder
as students fall in Iran and Thailand,
as Africa and Israel explode,
as cheap imitations fell Irish children,
or as, right here,
the jobless riot, and are crushed.
These are clean-handed killers,
emotionless, computerized,
distant from the screams
of tortured and dying.

Shel Horowitz

AUGUST 6TH, 1978

Clearly, God is on our side.
The only time all day
it didn't rain
was as we marched,
with candles,
to the U.N.

By our flickers, we can read
the Isaiah Wall:
   And they shall beat their swords
into plowshares,
their spears into pruning hooks.
Nation shall not rise against nation.
Neither shall they make war
anymore.

Candles pay tribute
to the tortured, the dead.
We affirm the living:
No more wars, no more bombs.
The easy part was convincing God;
Leaders need more work.

Shel Horowitz

DEAD WRONG

It is night; the bomb
has fallen.
Here was our mistake:
we marched, but not
to the arsenals.

We never went in, tools in hand,
to dismantle what should never
have been built.
In Russia, it will always
be night.
Tomorrow, our own lights
go out.

This is the way the world ends...
this is the way the world ends...
not with a whimper,
with a bang.

Shel Horowitz

HUMAN BEINGS...
AN ENDANGERED SPECIES
(*Fellowship of Reconciliation*)

NEITHER YOU NOR I NOR CHILDREN
THE ILL NOR THE LILIES OF THE FIELD
HARVEST NOR PLANTING NOR
THE WORKS OF SHAKESPEARE
BLOOD OF MARTYRS NOT THE
HEROISM OF PRISONERS
OF BUDDHISM NOT THE SOUNDING
THE GREEN MEMORY OF GANDHI
MARTIN KING NO NOR THE HOPE
OF THE THOUGHTFUL THE SOLITUDES

Dear Friends (September 1978)

There is the good news that 13 of us were arrested at the pentagon on Friday Sept. 1. We will be tried on various charges on
Sept. 15. The informed prediction is that some of us will receive
30-60 days. . . The sweet cheat against the earth goes on. The
authorities seem transfixed, there is much chatter and little
wisdom. We would pray to be accounted among the wise (or at
least the less unwise). At least to the extent that we are not cogs
in the engine of Armageddon.

Peace to you, and every blessing.

Daniel Berrigan

HOLY CONTEMPLATIVES · NONE OF THESE
THEIR PLANS ARE CONSUMMATED IF THEIR
OCCURS · THEY WOULD DECLARE GOD A
AN CASUALTY THIS IS WHAT I MAKE OF

NOR tHe UNBORN NOR tHe aged NOR
    NOR tHe FiSH OF tHe sea NOR
SKieS NOT SeasONS NOR
    OR DaNte OT PicaSSO NOR tHe
tEARS OF eXiLeS NOT tHe
    NOT tHe COHEReNt HONEYcomB
    VaULt OF CHRiStiANity NOt
    NOR tHe ROLLiNJ tHUNDeRS OF
WHICH FUELS US tHe LONJ SavaNNas
iNHaBiteD HeRe aND tHERe BY

Dear Friends (August 1979)

On Hiroshima Day, eleven of us were arrested at the notorious
Riverside Research Insititute, a pentagon think tank, here in
Manhattan. We were part of an all day vigil; and at noon during a
liturgy of repentance, we sat down in front of the doors and poured copious quantities of human blood. We will have our day in
court on September 19. . . The Institute, ironically and fittingly,
is located in a deteriorating neighborhood quite typical of the
city. There it squats exacting its tribute of human misery, its
'inventive dwarfs' (Brecht) passing in and out to do their thing.
Surely we witness here the dead end of science gone mad.

On the eighth of August, I journeyed to Washington to be with
folk for the day of mourning for Nagasaki. On the 9th, we poured
blood and ashes, cuffed outselves to the doors; and at noon did a
'die in' in the main concourse. There was prayer and fury and
hope in the air, and I am grateful.

We are told that such events as these occurred in some hundred cities during these days. Dare we hope that an awakening is
occurring across the land, parallel to that which eventually made
the Vietnam war unwageable?

We are planning for 1980, a continuous presence at the
pentagon, made up of groups from around the country. For all of
us, the pentagon is not merely a moral affront on the Potomac; it
is a tentacled monster ruling our economy, tainting our bread,
corrupting mothers' milk, claiming our sanctuaries. An unholy
Spirit, reaching in defiance of holiness, to 'the joining place of
soul and body.' Let us draw the nuclear blade, and be healed.

Warmth and light,

Dan Berrigan

NOT ONe iS SAFe NOtHiN9 iS SAFe iF
    WeaPONS aRe Lit iF MiSCHANCe
NONENtitY aFiJMeNT a BiJ BONe iN
OUR PReDiCAMeNt

255

Banner displayed on the White House Lawn. A similar banner—in Russian—was unfurled simultaneously in Red Square.

Karl Bissenger

MISSION TO MOSCOW

In newspapers around the world it was reported that on Labor Day, September 4, 1978, Soviet police broke up a disarmament demonstration by a group of American tourists in Red Square.

In Washington, a simultaneous demonstration at the White House was stopped by Secret Service agents. The demonstrators in both cities were members of the War Resisters League. All 13 persons arrested in Moscow, including newsmen and other tourists, were briefly detained and released without charges. The 11 demonstrators arrested in Washington were jailed, charged with unlawful entry, sent to trial and found guilty and threatened with six months in prison.

In both super-power capitals, the protesters handed out leaflets [in English and Russian] calling for nuclear weapons disarmament. "Our governments have talked of peace while preparing for war," said one leaflet. "Our governments have spoken eloquently of developing the human potential and meeting human needs while wasting our nations' wealth in an insane arms race."

The issue was put, perhaps, even more starkly in a subsequent pamphlet by the War Resisters League, noting that this was only the latest in a series of antiwar actions bridging East and West by various peace groups:

"While Soviet and American leaders heckle each other over who is responsible for the arms race, or over who more deeply violates human rights, these two super powers move steadily closer to the brink of nuclear war. Nuclear war by accident or by the act of a politically irrational leader. . .

"Nuclear war is the final crime. No matter how evil you may think the Soviet Union is, nothing it has done in its entire history would be as criminal, or as great a violation of human rights, as the destruction of every man, woman, and child in that nation by nuclear weapons.

"The real issue is not pinning down who is responsible for the arms race. The real issue is finding out who is responsible enough to end it. *Now.*"

So, while the great important powers of the world are piling up arms, nuclear armaments—all the noise and terror of coming war—we did a small, quiet kind of simple thing. We stepped out onto the grass of our own president's public home and our friends unfurled a banner in the public place of Russian power and we said Listen! Stop!

Whatever you decide about us—guilty or not guilty—we hope you hear what we're saying. Otherwise you'll be taking risks much greater than we've taken and the grass of the whole world will be dangerous. . .

Grace Paley

*in a statement to the court not permitted
by the judge to be made to the jury.*

AT THE MAIN GATE, GENERAL DYNAMICS, GROTON

The *U. S. Ohio*, the first Trident submarine,
is to be baptized. Its long
blunt red tube still lies in the ways.
"They have to paint it gray yet."
"Can't let it in the water yet."
Launched, loosed into the water,
it will be able
with 408 atomic bombs
to extinguish almost all life in a few minutes
in any country.
　　　Thirty-five hundred protesters watch
celebrant workers and townspeople entering
the main gate. Those entering
step over sitting-down protesters.
There is a sobering
unity of silence as the hundreds go in.
And come out, and again
must pass those watching.
State police push the watchers back. A sign:
THE U.S. OHIO IS A SIN.
Behind the sign, a young woman
is carrying a little girl.
A week before Easter, the temperature
is forty-three. It is like winter.
The mother wraps a blanket
around her child who shivers, batting eyes
with a not happy expression. The watchers now,
including the young mother,
in low voices begin to sing,
"All we are asking is give peace a chance.
All we are asking is give peace a chance."
The repeated, soft, predominantly alto
song follows the celebrants leaving.
The little girl asks her mother,
"Can they hear us?"

Millen Brand

SALT II

The
fac
par
pro
hor
pre
dan
sti
pea
or
the
off
cog
sen
in
anx
sta
pop
com
phi
obv
fac
pol
men
ext

Paul Eugene Clark

AFSC/FOR ROCKY FLATS PROJECT •

OCTOBER 15, 1978

Nine Minutes til Doomsday and
the Movement is Growing

Shivering with the terror of a stillborn idea—
more past, than before, its time,
the vigil waits and watches uneasily
for the windy morning to blow itself out
against the sunlit clouds of midday.
Hands keep grasping for positive signs—
paper crucifixes to ward off Reality's vampire.
Must even the end wear a smile?
Empty as the hollow stump of a dead tree,
I stand my post as the passers-by calculate my age
by counting the layers of self-doubt
riddled sphinxlike across a granite forehead.
A baby in the infancy of resistance
peeks out over the blue-woolen edge
of his world's cuddled beginning
at the radiant sky-crack of breaking day.
My worried eyes cast a shadow
over the drooling chin of this precocious visionary
who laughs at the comic cloud above
while I stare blankly into the tempest below.

Paul Eugene Clark

PETITION

We the living who desire not to die
      surprised by radiant fire
hurled without warning from the depths of space
      by robot rocketeers.
we who would voyage with our fellows on earth.
      nor fear the innocent skies.
address the ambassadors of the divided house
and their overlords in the chambers of power:

O masters of those who know the secret of secrets,
      guardians of good and evil,
do not divide the atom to give each of the living
      a fragmentary death;
divide it so each may inherit a portion of life
      sweeter than any yet known,
divide it so each may share the good news
      of a common earth and sky.

O fumbling masters of mystery:
      make chain-reactions
not of bright destruction to blind the last
      small witness-eye of heaven;
make chain-reactions of enlightenment
      to spread from man to man;
restore our broken alphabets of hope
and unite our fading vision in a new
      and healing stream of light.

Open the doors of our tombs today,
      open the doors to tomorrow,
before the eyeless are stoned by the blind:
      do not deny our petition!
Let this letter be signed by young and old
      in all our doomed towns and villages;
Let our voices be heard in the chambers of power,
and in the darkening chambers of each man's heart...

Cornel Lengyel

SOME TOMORROWS

(scenes from an unfinished future)

i   dunes and craters
left over from the last war

a gas of a war for those who sat in shelters
while helter-skelter over their heads
ran the dispossessed but not disenchanted
(who had least been able to escape it
had known longest it was bound to come)

and the others sipped their martinis
watched the big screen
and were surprised

ii   the molar men and women wriggled
out of their tubes and laughed
at that funny man
            einstein
saying world war four would
            be fought with bows and arrows:
here they were, safe
        and sound from world war
            seven (or five,
by the new reckoning) and the weaponry had been
          been twice
               (at least)

as sophisticated as
that of the previous war

iii   —and the five hundred years
they'd spent in the tubes
had let the farmlands
grow clean again
or so they thought—

iv   love conquered
finally
in 6337
and it was heard to remember
the time that went before

v   Berdie had speared a rat that day and was cooking it. Outside
the circle of the fire, hungry eyes watched. The rats were
still afraid of the fire, but they were getting bigger.

vi   When we opened the hatches,
bones clattered in;
forgotten ancestors
implored us one last time
for shelter.

Douglas Michael Massing

WAR DISEASE

It's a slow/angry/loving process, waging peace, overcoming the
plain rational fact that you can't be peaceful and survive.
Which is true. Just as true as it was in the 13th Century
that infectious disease was the will of the Lord. Exactly so
until people learned how disease worked (and this is in no way
to diminish the workings of any Lord, either)...

Tom Hawkins

FOR WHY else would MEN MAKE WAR but they might be MOTHERS too and have LIFE TO HOLD IN THEIR ARMS

Kathleen Stillwell

COMBATING THE LOVE OF WAR

Shortly after I got out of the army, I placed my dress uniforms in the Salvation Army box, and I mailed my service ribbons, combat medical badge, and minor decorations back to the Pentagon. One of the reasons I returned the decorations was to protest the war in Vietnam, but I had other motivation. I have always thought it rather pathetic when veterans put on their old dress uniforms with their medals pinned to their chests. It appears that the vets are wallowing in nostalgia, trying to relive the most exciting part of their lives and forgetting what the war was really like. In me are the seeds for that kind of illusory retrospection and I wanted to avoid it. The irony is that I gave away the uniforms and the decorations, but I cannot, nor do I want to, give away the memories.

Several years ago, Ed McCurdy wrote a song in which he described the strangest dream he had ever known—that men had come together to put an end to war. I believe that putting an end to war will continue to remain the strangest dream unless we can understand why men go off to war.

Contrary to popular rhetoric, men do not go to war because it is kill or be killed. Certainly our country was in no physical danger by what happened in a few small countries in Southeast Asia. The United States had learned to live with the fact that China has gone Communist; obviously, a Communist Vietnam, Cambodia, and Laos represent no threat to us.

It is also my strong belief that wars are not caused primarily by the need for territorial expansion, political freedom, material gain, to save democracy, or to preserve peace. We in Vietnam did not fight for apple pie, the right to boo the umpire, or for the freckled-faced girl next door.

At the beginning of *To Hell and Back* Audie Murphy wrote that whatever happened, it was his own fault for he had always wanted to be a soldier. In *Soldier*, Anthony Herbert said that as a ten-year-old he cried when his two brothers went off to war because he could not go with them. During World War II, (Gen.) George Patton wrote to his wife that he loved war and dreaded the thought of peace. Ward Just tells of an interview with a West Point graduate who prayed the war in Vietnam would not end until he had a chance to get there. As an adolescent I had occasional regrets that I had been too young to be in the Korean War.

It is easy to look at the war in Vietnam and know why one should hate it—people killed and crippled, homes destroyed, land bombed, countryside defoliated. What is infinitely more difficult is to articulate why I loved it.

One of the problems of war may be that our memories deceive us. In reality most of soldiering is quite dull, and of my 300 days in Vietnam I was probably in combat less than forty-eight hours. Yet when I reflect on my tour of duty there, I perceive it as the most exciting period of my life. Just as mothers frequently forget about the pain, and view childbirth as a beautiful experience, we soldiers forget the horror of war and remember only the excitement.

To me the fundamental attraction of war is not the spectacular sights that one sees, but the intensity of feeling that is involved. Perhaps part of this feeling of intensity in war is a function of the fact that most soldiers are young, and youth are liable to feel intensely about a great number of things. However, I do not believe youth is a total explanation for this intensity.

There is intensity in war because death is so imminent that one grasps for each moment because it may be the last. Time becomes like a damp washcloth that one takes and wrings out in an attempt to squeeze out every bit of living that life offers in the present moment. In the space of only a few seconds, one can feel terror and then ecstasy. These contrary feelings and experiences are compressed together in such a way that it is as if one lived a lifetime in only a few months.

Even if one day there exists no economic or political injustice, war will continue to be a present reality as long as the majority of us feel that our lives are boring and meaningless. A basic question is why we flee to war to provide ourselves with fulfillment. Why should the desire for intensity be met in the act of destructive violence?

I believe useless destruction to be morally wrong, and I have done enough reading about the politics of Vietnam to believe our involvement there was a political mistake from the very beginning. Yet along with these beliefs was my desire to be in a war. I believe much of my own anti-war activity was the result of my attempt to exorcise those feelings of pleasure that I experienced in Vietnam.

Patton rationalized his enthusiastic participation in war with the belief that war is inevitable; therefore, man should resign himself to it and welcome war as a manly challenge. I recoil from the idea of accepting such fatalism, but I must admit I do not know what can provide human beings' peacetime lives with such a sense of meaning and fulfillment that they will not seek out war.

A step in the right direction is for us to admit publicly that we love, not hate, war. Once we admit that we love war, perhaps we can develop a realistic understanding of our sinfulness. If we confront our sin, then one day the strangest dream may no longer be a dream but a reality.

Harrison Kohler

COUNTER-RECRUITMENT

Smiling faces from the storefront window

85 reasons to join

the pitch
        is no longer

                    a masculine identity
16 feminine smiles
            broadcast
       the economic pinch
            persuasively
            hint
       at seductive treasures
            prophesize
       a fatalistic cure
                    for the boredom
                         the frustration
                         the pain
learn a trade!
                              travel!
            Kill.....
            Time.....
                         and all sense of reason
       can not restore the lost identity
Smith-Rodriguez-Alvarez-Brown-Mendoza
            burnt flesh
sizzling
            in the sunlight of future wars
discarded ideals-
            words shot at the enemy
            with deadly force
       their true meaning
            left smoking in the dirt

visions of hope
            shrouded in a cloud
                         of radioactive
                         debris-
limited.....
       offensive.....
                         to the minds
of beings still endowed with hearts
            bleeding
            bleeding
       for peace
                    carry the lantern
                    carry the dead
       turn from the beguiled smiles
                         with speed
                    and all good conscience
            and seek

            peace

Cliff Catton

FOR A U.S. PEACE ACADEMY

"We have grasped the mystery of the atom and rejected the Sermon on the Mount. . . .Ours is a world of nuclear giants and ethical infants. We know more about war than we know about peace, more about killing than we know about living."

—General Omar Bradley, Chief of Staff,
U.S. Army; Boston, November 10, 1948.

War, these days, is complicated enough, but peace—? Perhaps the clearest way to express it is to say that peace is to war what chess is to checkers—they are both played on the same board, but peace is infinitely more complex than war.

And these days I often find myself wishing some of my fellow workers in the cause of peace would somehow come to grips with the complexity of the problem, because the acceptance of that complexity is the first step toward its solution. I understand there are over 2,000 active peace organizations in this country, and each of them has its own agenda. What pains me is the overly simplistic thinking on which many of those agenda are based. I submit to you, for example, that a program based on the slogan "Full and complete disarmament now!" is hardly an exercise in realism, given the very dangerous world in which we live. It is simply a fact—again, in the absence of divine intervention—that peace is not going to spring forth full-blown, like Minerva from the brow of Jove! Peace is going to be built like any great sturdy monument, one brick at a time, each brick resting on those laid before by builders all down through the ages.

It is this latter kind of thinking that has produced the Peace Academy concept. Once the immense complexity of the problem of peace is accepted, then we can attack it like any other complex problem—by breaking it down into simpler parts and working out solutions to those parts one at a time. That is the approach which produces the answers that in time will solve the more complex problem, and those individual answers are the bricks which will eventually build man's most long-sought monument—a stable peace for the world.

We should all put up on our walls the ancient Oriental quotation: "Better to light one candle than to curse the darkness." And second, I think we should do those many things which we can do on a gradual, patient basis to build the foundation for a permanent peace and assist those who are working to do so, always keeping in mind President Kennedy's statement to the United Nations when he said, "Peace is a daily, a weekly, a monthly process, gradually changing opinions, slowly eroding old barriers, quietly building new structures." My point is that we are involved in literally changing the world, in changing our whole cultural bias and heritage, and it is no job for the faint of heart!

Peace—all nations seek it! The search for peace is at least as old as the Judeo-Christian ethical tradition. All religions exalt it and cherish it among their highest values. Remember the fourth chapter of Micah: "They shall beat their swords into ploughshares and prepare for war no more;" and then of course comes the New Testament, much of it devoted to proclaiming the message and the search for peace on earth.

Peace—all people yearn for it; every public opinion poll shows it is at the top of everybody's "want list," yet in the words of Patrick Henry, "Gentlemen may cry peace, but there *is* no peace," and, we might add, no visible progress towards any lasting peace. We have had 150 wars since the end of World War II in 1945. Today in the world there are somewhere between 40 and 50 wars in progress.

Since 1945—since the end of World War II—military spending around the globe has exceeded six trillion dollars, that is, 6,000 billion dollars! That is about $1500 for each human being alive on the earth today, man, woman and child. And since 1960, world military expenditures are up 60%, and despite mushrooming fire-power capabilities, the number of the world's Armed Forces are also up 20%!

We like to think we are a peaceful people, but the U.S. nuclear arsenal contains enough destructive power to equal 700,000 Hiroshimas, or the equivalent of more than three tons of TNT for each person! I think that's probably enough, because some of those persons are really very small.

We are a peaceful people, yet we have four excellent military academies and at least five war colleges, all dedicated to maintaining peace by armed force. Is it unreasonable to suggest that we might have one national institution devoted to teaching and research in how to create conditions of peace by affirmative means? It's not a very comforting comment, but it was a wise man who recently wrote, "In the normal course of events, nations get what they prepare for."

Confucius, while visiting in the state of Wei, was asked what he would do first if he were requested to head the government of that country, and he replied, "As a first step I would see to it that things were called by their right names, for if things are not called by their right names then the statements are misleading, and when the statements are misleading then nothing can be accomplished."

So let's start off by calling things by their right names. For example, "national security"—what is it? Well, for 200 years "national security" meant the ability to defend ourselves and our friends in the event of the next war bursting upon us. So we built up our armed forces and trained the world's best military leaders and experts. But the world has a way of changing the scenery while we're watching the show, and suddenly those same experts tell us that no real defense is possible in a modern thermonuclear attack. If modern war is forced upon us, there is no defense to be made. And thus, suddenly "national security"—called by its right name—means not *preparing* for war, but *avoiding* it.

But what is the next step in that logic of right-naming? Obviously, if "national security" means developing the ability to avoid war, we should be training not only military experts—that is, experts in making war—but also experts in all sorts of peace-making, in avoiding war. Thus we should be training experts in non-violent conflict resolution—in non-military crisis intervention—in creating the conditions of peace—in analyzing social systems in terms of their peace potential.

What do we mean when we say "peace"? In conflict resolution terms, peace is not defined as the absence of all conflict. As long as people are less than perfect, conflict is probably unavoidable and even necessary in our society. We need it if we are to have any change or progress—it's the yeast or the leaven, the engine of change, the mechanism of progress. Without it the inertia of the status quo becomes overwhelming.

But conflict need not lead to violence. In the field of conflict resolution, peace is defined as the non-violent management of conflict.

Well, I'm asked, conflict resolution sounds great, but does it work? Yes—you can bet it works—in fact, you probably know a dozen cases where it has worked:

—it worked during the Hanafi Muslim takeover in Washington, where experts in conflict resolution got involved early and probably saved fifty hostages' lives;

—it worked at Wounded Knee, where expert intervention prevented the already violent FBI-Indian confrontation from developing into the last great Indian war. . .

—it worked recently at Kent State University, where the violence of similar events ten years ago was avoided;

—it has worked in over 100 prison riot situations in the past two years, which were resolved by the professionals of the Community Relations Service using conflict resolution techniques, so that the riots never reached the stage of head-lines in the newspapers; the opposite case occurred at Attica in New York in 1971, where attempts to resolve the conflict miscarried because no experts in conflict resolution were involved, and the result was a massacre with 43 dead—and a national disgrace.

—it worked in Miami in 1972 where the violence of the Chicago 1968 Democratic Convention was avoided at both the Democratic and Republican Conventions due to the carefully orchestrated intervention of large numbers of experts in conflict resolution;

—we all saw it work at least an initial minor miracle of peace-making at Camp David, where President Carter gave us a prime example of mediative techniques—and their superiority over traditional diplomacy in achieving progress toward the settlement of international disputes.

Recently, my own Pastor, George Booth, in Arlington, Virginia, told the story in a sermon of the great Quaker, John Woolman, who by gentle persuasion rid the Society of Friends of the Curse of Slavery long before the Civil War. Then George asked: "What if there had been 500 John Woolmans?" Yes, what if? What might have been accomplished without the terrible tragedy of Shiloh and Wilderness and Gettysburg—and the one hundred years of repetitious tragedy which were their aftermath in the South? But now, what if the Peace Academy can be founded and turn out ten thousand experts in Conflict Resolution between 1980 and the year 2000?

What if other countries not only send their best and brightest students to the Peace Academy, but also emulate us and start their own Peace Academies? They will, you know; already four foreign countries have expressed interest.

Oftentimes recently, while speaking on the Peace Academy concept in various areas of the country, I have been challenged by skeptics who say, ''Oh, come on now—human beings have always fought and always will. We've always had wars, and we always will. How can Conflict Resolution change human nature?''

One response to that is merely to pose a couple of equally well-founded questions, such as : ''Mankind has always structured his society to assure racial survival, not annihilation. Why do you think the atomic age will change those rules? Survival of the species is the first great law of nature—why do you think it has now been repealed?''

But I think it is perhaps enough to point out that although war is indeed an ancient and honored human institution, it is not sacrosanct. History demonstrates that human institutions are normally cherished long after they become anachronisms, but they are abandoned when, and only when, they become either useless or counter-productive. War has now achieved that distinction. I really think we have arrived at a genuine conjunction of history when war, which has always been evil, has now become useless; and mankind, however much it may seem to be attracted to recognized evil, is instinctively repelled by any institution which is thoroughly and demonstrably useless—or uselessly destructive.

Milton C. Mapes

THE AGE OF THE SOLDIER

I have an 18 year old son. Viet Nam
to his generation is ancient history.

So now as you grow
to the age of the soldier
I am amazed, I am unbelieving
that any mother
has ever given
her son
to the bloodstained hands of war.

Sharon Doubiago

CRY WOLF

(on the re-institution of draft
registration: July 21st, 1980)

Again the clarion cries across the land:
To arms! The British are coming!
The Persians are coming.
The Russians are almost here.

Athletes and wheat are banned from Moscow,
but computer sales continue;
public schools are an utter disgrace,
but the government wants
fifty-six billion more dollars
for an MX nuclear shell game—
and now you offer your children up
without so much as a whimper,
believing in God
knows what:

Whose side are you on, anyway?

The beliefs worth dying for
are not the ones practiced
by the people who order your children
to die for them.

W.D. Ehrhart

ANOTHER NAPOLEON'S MARCH ON MOSCOW?

Napoleon Bonaparte once boasted that because of his conscription system he could afford to lose 25,000 soldiers a month.

25,000 human beings killed, wounded, or crippled each month. For Napoleon, they were a mere impediment to his success, to be replaced by a draft call.

Terrible as that figure is, however, it is small by today's standards. The army which Napoleon led on Moscow numbered 400,000. Today's U.S. military recruits that many in a year. If there were a mobilization, the Pentagon calculates that it would need that many new conscripts after six weeks of fighting.

In all of the discussion about the draft, it is easy to lose sight of people. The conscription mindset thinks not of people at all, but of replacements...

That's why it is good to sit, as I did just yesterday, and open the mail that comes to CCCO. There has been a lot of it recently, and all of it from people—not replacements. A sixteen-year-old who worries that there will be an active draft by the time she is old enough. A mother of two sons of draft age. A young man in California whose neatly-typed letter is an eloquent plea for peace.

Opening the mail reminds me that these people, their future and the future of their world, are what the draft debate is really all about.

Bob Seeley

from MY MIND SAYS NO!

Many things I do not understand;
But I know that while
People suffer neglect-hunger-pain
There is a place called
THE PENTAGON,
And that is never
HUNGRY!
Money that could care for us,
Feed us, house us
Is given to the greedy PENTAGON
Where bigger and better
And costlier ways
To KILL
Are planned.

Is it more important
To kill than
To care?
So I, a tired old woman,
And many more
Tired old people
Will stay
And tell what we know.

When we die
There will be more of us...
Many, many more.

We will find officials
Who think people
Are important —
More important
Than that place called
THE PENTAGON.

We will find officials
Who think it is more important
To care
Than to kill.

Janet N. Neuman

ADDRESS TO MIDDLE AMERICA

This speech was delivered as an *Address to the Members of Pebble Hill Church, Doylestown, Pennsylvania, on June 1, 1980.*

In the fall of 1976, I visited a journalism class at Pennridge High School in Perkasie, PA, to talk about the Vietnam war. The first question I was asked was whether or not the anti-war movement in the United States had affected my morale while I was fighting in Vietnam.

I told the students that it had not, though we could not help being aware of the demonstrations. What had damaged our morale, I told them, was the discovery that the people we had been sent to defend did not want us there—and indeed, more often than not and with good reason, hated us; that we had been ordered by our government to win the hearts and minds of the people of Vietnam with nothing but rifles and bombs and American arrogance; that what we were involved in had nothing to do with the cause of freedom and democracy and liberty for which I had enlisted in 1966 at the age of 17; that we were Redcoats, not patriots, and that our national leaders had put us up to it; that we were killing and dying for something worse than nothing.

275

My answer fell on blank faces. After class was dismissed, the teacher who had invited me said that the kids had never heard anything like what I had said, that they were being taught in history class that America lost the war in Vietnam because the anti-war movement had undermined the morale of the soldiers and broken their will to win. The silence of the students, he said, was the silence of confusion and disbelief.

In 1977, I taught at the University of Illinois. One day I happened to mention Dean Rusk. Again, silence. I asked the class of 22 college freshmen and sophomores who Dean Rusk was. Not only could no one tell me—none of them had ever heard the name.

In 1978, I taught at a Quaker high school in Maryland. In one class, we were studying the poet Phillip Appleman and I assigned five of Appleman's poems dealing with Vietnam. The next day, 16-year-old Liza Feeney began the class by asking "Do we have to talk about this stuff?"

"Why don't you want to talk about it, Liza?" I asked.

"It's so depressing," she replied. "Why can't we talk about his love poems? They make me feel good."

"Do you know what happened in Vietnam?" I asked.

"We lost a war," she responded hesitantly. It was almost a question.

"What do you mean?" I asked. She shook her head slowly. She didn't have anything else she could add. Clearly, the only thought she could address the question with was the burning desire to have had the sense to keep her mouth shut in the first place.

"Do you know where Vietnam is, Liza?" A pause.

"Someplace in Asia, I think," she said, finally. "Isn't it?"

Last fall, I went to a Vanderbilt football game. At halftime, a group of students came onto the field with an effigy of Ayatollah Khomeini hanging from a pole and a large banner reading "Nuke Iran." They were clearly having a good time.

It's eerie. It is awesome and frightening. It is 1984 four years ahead of schedule. It is as though the events of the past 15 years never happened. A catastrophic event that bent my life 180 degrees, a crime so grotesque I had thought the flag-waving myth of Duty-Honor-Country could never again be resurrected from its well-deserved grave, is as remote and irrelevent to the newest generation of potential cannon-fodder as are the civilizations of ancient Crete and Mycenae.

Is it possible that we have learned absolutely nothing? Is it even within the realm of imagination that we could so desecrate the memories of Khe Sanh and My Lai and Con Thien and Kent State and Jackson and Chicago? Are we really willing to allow another generation of children to march to their deaths for the pride of powerful men and the dividends of IBM and Exxon and Gulf & Western and Transamerica and Lockheed and Dow and Dupont?

And yet our children are ignorant. They know only what they have been taught—at home, in school, in the newspapers, on television, in church, at Boy Scouts and Girl Scouts, and the thousand other places and ways I learned the pigeon-breasted fantasies that filled my head the day I took the Oath of Allegiance and joined the United States Marine Corps thinking my sacrifice was a glorious gesture overflowing with grandeur and nobility.

We have taught our children nothing. We have wrapped ourselves in the shame of our complicity and the pain of our own shattered illusions and the fear of reprobation from our neighbors and friends and colleagues and associates, and allowed our children's preceptions of the world to be dictated by *The Deer Hunter* and *The Daily Intelligencer* and the press releases of Jody Powell.

Secretary of Defense Harold Brown catalogues the list of Russian evils in Afghanistan: helicopter gunships, wholesale search and seizure, napalm, aerial gas—and it's like hearing a re-cap of American Indochina—and he insists that such atrocities cannot be tolerated by a peace-loving American people. The same Harold Brown who was Secretary of the Air Force during the war in Vietnam. And we remain silent.

For humanitarian reasons, Jimmy Carter invites a broker of misery and oppression—a billionaire with a fortune built out of his people's blood and our tax dollars—to come to an American hospital, and when the people of Iran get angry, Carter expresses astonishment and outrage, exhorting his subjects to rally 'round the flag. And we remain silent.

The Defense Department is about to construct a nuclear shellgame in the deserts of Utah and Nevada in the form of the $56 billion MX Missile System while the food stamp program limps precariously from month to month and the price of hamburger soars over $1.50 a pound and our schools—already overcrowded and understaffed—teeter on the brink of bankruptcy. And we remain silent.

Our own representative in Congress, Peter H. Kostmayer, says "clearly we have to take a strong stand against the Soviet invasion of Afghanistan" and "fully support(s)" the Olympic boycott and a "5.2 percent increase above inflation" in the 1981 defense budget, stating that we must "demonstrate to the Soviets that we mean to protect our interests overseas." And we remain silent.

Has anybody asked himself lately whose interests overseas are going to be protected? Has anybody asked himself lately, when the draft notices begin arriving in the mail—and they will begin arriving, whether it be next week or next month or next year—who will be ordered to protect those interests?

I can tell you who. Not the children of Robert McNamara, who is now president of the World Bank. Not the children of Dean Rusk, who is now Sibley Professor of International Law at the University of Georgia. Not the children of Clark Clifford, who is now director of Phillips Petroleum Company. Not the children of McGeorge Bundy, who is now president of the Ford Foundation. Not the children of Harold Brown or Edmund Muskie or Jimmy Carter or Ronald Reagan or Edward Kennedy.

Our children are going to be ordered to protect those interests, that's who. Your children and my children. And the interests they will be fighting and killing and dying for won't be yours or mine or theirs.

And what have we given our children with which they might defend themselves against the stirring false words and shining false values utterly believed by false men and women who would make of a nation born of revolution and liberty a nation of sheep and followers?

Can we really afford to remain silent? Do we care so little for the next generation, and the one after that, and the one after that? Does it really cost more than we are willing to bear to teach our children the truth? Real patriotism often requires sacrifices greater than blood and obedience, and real love knows no price too high.

"Are you now contented to let....dissembling, insinuating men...carry their point against you, when you can, with infinitely more ease and safety, counterwork them...?" asked Christopher Gadsden, organizer of South Carolina's Sons of Liberty, in 1769. "Only be roused from your sleep; dare to see the truth, to support the truth; and the God of Truth will make you free."

And if we fail to dare, who will wear the shackles of our failure?

W.D. Ehrhart

REMEMBERING KENT

They carried heavy rifles,
Loaded with deadly missiles
    Able to tear the soul from a body at three thousand yards.
These weapons made Goliaths of the smallest men.
Against this army of Philistines
    Only a handful of would-be Davids
    Lobbed their ill-aimed stones.

The dwindled crowd dispersed,
The soldiers turned and marched up a hill,
    Glancing back as they marched,
    Falling out of formation,
Keeping in view the scattering youths they left behind.

As if on a signal, on cresting the hill,
The vanguard of executioners
    Wheeled,
    Retraced their last few steps,
And launched the attack against the youths they had left behind,
Now a hundred yards away.
    Turning first in wonder,
Other soldiers eagerly joined the fusilade.
        Thirteen bloodied students lying;
        Grass and asphalt red;
    Four of thirteen dead or dying,
        Slaughtered as they fled.
    Seeing then the scene their fury
        To the world displayed,
    Soldiers — shaken — turned and hurried
        Off the other way.

Remember this
    A decade after;
Remember Kent. . .
    And cry!

    Cry for the nation
That turned the arms of an insolent war
    Against her own children;
That rained the fury of her war-born hatred
    Upon herself;
And tried to escape the shame of her madness
    By turning her eyes away.

Cry tears of mourning;
    Of outrage;
    Of warning. . .
But cry not the tears of despair!
Cry out in voices resolved against silence,
Determined to speak for those silenced at Kent!
Cry out for justice!
    For peace!
    For compassion!
Cry out in loud voices,
    Remembering Kent!

David Engdahl

BLACK WINTER

...for a coming time...the boys have memories.
— Jeffers

1
The time between us stretches out
like a winter, lingering farther from the heart,
heavy as fourteen thousand miles of jet and rails.
Looking out, I can't tell whether the glass is crusted
with frost or if the land is beyond it, a white
face of resistance. The train from Malmo thrashes
the butcher-cold sleepers, drives me through the
gut of frozen landscape like a knife. Deep fog
so early. Us. Where can we meet anyone now except
on the edge of ice, anywhere so long as it isn't a jungle.

2
They said that Stockholm would make mortician
slabs of us American boys, cold and rootless. In
Montreal the summer before, underground
looking east and north, I met Charles X with you.
''Bright California black boy. He'll get everything right
in Sweden.'' And at first he was a fad in Lund, you
said, easy to get dates, domestic jobs like we all
needed. Then the exile's disease, common guilts,
assault, journalist's ink. Lost the same as if
in a jungle, you said. Everyday the papers full
of butchery. ''Oriental rubbish swept into a
pile by black & white GIs.'' But here she's sweet,
he'd say. ''She's Swedish pastry. No war and sweet
times.'' Someone else's car, six months into exile, a
yellow piece of dress, black billows, and just
small, American, Black rubbish on the ice.

3
First night we sat and watched the Swedish hospital burn,
bullhorn, glare of fire, lights, long engines —
imagining a jungle we'd both escaped beyond Honolulu.
''Exiles should stay out of the sun,'' you said laughing,
our breasts cold and tight so far north even self-
preservation froze. ''Along the circle, the Lapps dance
and chant stories through half a year of night, not
for entertainment but to keep from going crazy in the
darkness.'' The survivors here are fractured like cold
glass, bits of ghost in ice and heavy smoke. Wet, black
winter's going out. No one talks of escape.

4.
Out by the reef a low fire is burning on the sea,
and in the silent dark a color like old roses
is shining on the swells. When they'd burn off
the cover in those green jungles, the suffocating
small hills would crouch there beyond the flames
like these waves. Ten years beyond the war on this
wharf, I can justify almost nothing so simply as this
fire. The smell of petroleum burning and brine slams
me like a fist that strikes on a cold morning
and strikes again, insists and strikes until there's only
blood and burning through the nostrils. A black
mirror: ''One should watch and not speak. And patriotism
has run the world through so many blood-lakes: and
we always fall in…''

5
Near the far horizon the fire is out. The stars
blink on again through heavy smoke. The Pacific sea
extends again into space. And who did we leave
in the north like ice, and who did we leave there
in the south, scattered on the land like coal?

Frank Stewart

SUBSTITUTE HISTORY: On Holocaust Day

The Jews at Buchenwald look so
fashionable
with their cheekbones arching out of hollows
with their patched knees
that my daughter does not understand
those are women, not boys.
The coils of barbed wire look like
a hot dog wrapped to-go, she says
it looks solid.
I am teaching her heritage
admitting that my mother's mother's father
was a German
that he escaped conscription by emigrating
to Amerika, each brother
when he came of age —
there is no record of the sisters.
Patton ordered 1,000 civilians to Buchenwald
to look at mounds of bodies, they
walked through, eyes averted
stopped breathing
except to say: *We didn't know.*
Of the three million murdered gypsies
who were my father's cousins,
there is no record.

Susu Jeffrey

A WAR BABY REMEMBERS HITLER

34 years later there are some
who admire der Fuehrer
especially the ones who talk —
    he hated: snow
                fresh meat
                fresh air
                meat (after 1931)

                millions of
                Jews
                civilian life

282

liked women
and uniforms.

He took acting lessons from Charlie Chaplin.

He was a little guy
the Napoleon thing,
had a bad
    barber, temper,
a goosestep
sense of humor. His name
gives me goose flesh.

He technocraticized mass murder
divided the labor
so that each one could wash their hands
and sleep.

The SS
staying away from the front
getting rich playing
war
with starving sick prisoners
with gas bombs
and baton bullets
the unequal evil
of the chosen people vs. the master race
silhouetted against crematoria smokestacks
smogging, conveniently,
our view.

Many prayed.
The pope prayed.
The relatives prayed.
But most people
didn't believe
didn't believe
because it was legal.
All legal.
It was, in fact, the law.

Susu Jeffrey

REMEMBERING VIETNAM

This was the first war where Americans have not been able to go back to where they have fought. The whole thing, therefore, is insanely frozen in time.

Many of us deeply need contact with the reality of Viet Nam today, in order to work out the inner imprints of the war experience there. We need to see the people, the society, the land, the buildings, the paddies, the trees, and how they have changed with peace and reconstruction. We need to see in *that* way that the war is over; we need to see the land and the people now when we are free to look steadily, now that the eyes and ears do not have to be basically focused on the enemy and the danger, and the senses can fully register. There is a real land and people; we could not see it clearly then for the murky screen of war, and we cannot see it now in peace.

Contrast the situation with Europe or the Pacific after World War II or South Korea in the '50s. Not only could the veteran go there, but for the benefit of those who couldn't the post-war theaters were overrun with American journalists and photographers who provided a view of the face and evolution of the scenes of war experiences. We do not have that from Viet Nam either—no news, really, of the people and the land.

The most startling example of this has been the strange character of American reporting about the boat people. American journalists are writing from Hong Kong, Malaysia, remote islands of Indonesia, the Philippines, Hanoi even, but all the stories tell us is about the process of escape and the refugees' current life, plus, of course, diplomacy and conferences. But nothing about *Viet Nam*. It is as if they have sailed out from some black hole. Who are they? What towns are they from? What have they been doing since the war, since April 30, 1975? What did they do during the war? Who of us did they know then?...What has become of our Vietnamese friends? We don't know. Our journalists will not yet ask the boat people to talk, really talk, about life in Vietnam.

Along with the re-living of war experiences in dreams, there is a new kind now: portrayals of the places one was in Viet Nam as they might be now—attempts in dreams to fill in the historical gap, the space in time, to create images of the hills, paddies, villages, towns, military installations, rivers—as they might have evolved over the past several years; images of the American bases one lived and fought in, now aged a little, taken over by the Vietnamese, for new purposes, or reclaimed by the land. So some veterans dream on in search of a continuity of the place; we have been cut off from its history, and that hurts.

Especially anti-war veterans hate America still for what it did in Viet Nam. The hatred can be deep and abiding, and personally devastating. It may be confined to the issue of Viet Nam, but whether so confined or not, it seems permanent. Some exiles will never return; some will return physically but never emotionally. Some of us who were not exiles in body, are exiles in spirit, perhaps for life.

. . . .

Freeze-dried memories, quick flash-frozen memories, just add water—tears— and the original color, flavor, and consistency is restored. Or sometimes add just a little blood (rage)...Viet Nam veterans have many things locked up inside apart from grief—screaming, shaking, trembling, shivering, running away, lashing out, fire, atrocity, rage and hatred, all may be locked up inside...(Robert Jay) Lifton's concept of animating guilt suggests that we get well when we turn the experience of the war to good ends, become keepers of the garden.

There are many ways to use what was learned. One is to use what every Viet Nam veteran knows about the Third World, because of having lived in it, knows how power does not guarantee any wisdom at all about how to use it, to use such knowledge to work for peace in whatever corner of the world you can do that in.

Arthur S. Blank Jr.

THE GOOK-HUNTER

I have spent much of my adult life in Vietnam, and the United States as a journalist and documentary-film maker. I have been with American soldiers when they were killed or maimed. I admire America's admirable side and, like millions of Americans, harbor rational fears about its lethal side.

America is debating itself again on the Vietnam War. One movie has triggered this debate: "The Deer Hunter," which has won the best-picture Oscar and a fortune for its backers and makers. The debate has become something of a media event; indeed, it is approaching the point of obsolescence, with a "wrap-up" piece in a weekly newsmagazine. As if the truth should slip through by mistake, the author of that article says that how you view "The Deer Hunter's" image of the war depends on your politics. It does not. It depends on the truth. For no deluge of coffee-table intellectual inanities, such as "meaningful horror" and "metaphors of redemption," which film critics have written, will bend the truth of what happened over there.

America came out of Vietnam without a squeak from on high that what was done was wrong, that the war was a war of rampant technology against human beings. Perhaps that was understandable. The impression lingered and gained strength that it was all some unfortunate mistake, a mammoth bungle and no more.

For three years there was virtual silence. Then Hollywood sensed that a lot of money could be made with a movie that appealed directly to those racist instincts that cause wars and that allowed the Vietnam war to endure for so long—a movie that reincarnated the triumphant Batman-jawed Caucasian warrior, that presented the Vietnamese as Oriental brutes and dolts, that served up a new form of gratuitous violence in the orgiastic Russian-roulette scenes that never, to my knowledge, happened, and with John Wayne-like heroics and heavenly violins thrown in.

Nothing changes, it seems. This is how Hollywood created the myth of the Wild West, which was harmless enough unless you happened to be an American Indian, and how World War II and Korea were absorbed into box-office folklore, which was harmless enough unless you happened to be a "dumb Kraut" or an "unspeakable Nip" or a "Commie Chink," or one of a malleable generation and likely to be conditioned by simplistic images of war, a conditioning that caused many young Americans actually to embrace the war against the "Gooks." That the same cynical myth-making is now being applied to the most documented war in history, and that a cheap money-spinning travesty of a movie is being earnestly debated, induces more melancholy than anger in those like myself who saw whole Vietnamese communities used as guinea pigs for the testing of a range of "anti-personnel" military technology, and who saw demoralized, brutalized and often mutinous American teenagers lying in their own blood and excrement, for the purpose of some pointless, sacrificial siege staged in the cause of nothing, except the gratification of inept brass in their air-conditioned offices.

"The Deer Hunter" and its apologists insult the memory of every American who died in Vietnam. The myth-making went on this week: On Sunday, a prime-time drama about Vietnam, "Friendly Fire," was televised. With slickness and schmaltz, it salved everybody's guilt, especially the military's.

I went back to Vietnam last year. Much of the North, which few Americans ever saw, is a moonscape. All visible signs of life—houses, factories, schools, hospitals, pagodas, churches—have been obliterated. Forty-four percent of the forests have been destroyed; in many of those still standing there are no longer birds and animals.

There are thousands of children in Hanoi and Haiphong alone who are permanently deaf as a result of the bombing at Christmas 1972. More tons of bombs were dropped on Vietnam than were dropped during all of World War II. There are the deformed infants, damaged in the womb as a direct result of the poisoning of the landscape. There are the permanently dislocated and the insane, who ran from Gen. William Westmoreland's genocidal "free-fire zones." And there are the thousands of children fathered by Americans.

Several of them were singing this song when I visited a Saigon orphanage: "The war is gone. . . Planes come no more. . . Do not weep for those just born. . . The human being is evergreen." If you see "The Deer Hunter," you may want to remember these words.

John Pilger

THE WAR BETWEEN THE SEXES

Sometimes I understand the hatred of women
when in young soldiers I see
the mother's betrayal

Sometimes I hear women laughing
at the fathers who command
the son is coward
who follows the love
of the heart

Sometimes I see the mother as the true warrior
who raises the child
who refuses to fight
the father's childish war

Sometimes I see in women the end of all war
when in the father I see
his mother's betrayal

the father who thinks
to make a man
the mother who knows
that knowing who's boss
produces obedient lambs

Sometimes I understand the fear of my father
when in my daughter I see
Iphigenia
she who he would sacrifice
that war might begin

Sometimes I remember
Oedipus did not know
he was loving his mother

though ever since
men have made women afraid
of loving their sons

When in young boys I see the father's cold war:
young men turning
to young men for love

then I understand
the longing of the son

to touch
the father

When in young soldiers I see the mother's betrayal
she who let the Man
take her son as prisoner

she who is convinced:
gender is species
the male is another race
the father is distance
there is war
between the sexes
she is the weaker
and love will make him soft
and love will make him female
and love will make him
unfit for the world

then, sometimes, I understand
War, the mother who betrays her son
the one in whom he believed he was safe
Now who hands him over
to the bloodstained hands of war

In the womb-deep touch of mother I see
women going to war
the raising of sons
to the heart's battle

for the heart is the mind
the heart is the parent
the heart is the child
the heart is the country
the heart is
the man

Always I know
love is great enough

Sometimes I see
that women could raise
the only future we have
the lovers
we've always longed for

Sharon Doubiago

ANTIETAM TO VIETNAM

It was not the first
Nor the last
There were more famous battles
But it happened
It was real to those
Who got wounded there
Got maimed there
Died there
It was real for those who fought at Antietam

They will say
Some future day
It was all just an accident of involvement
Almost unreal a dream a nightmare
But it happened
It was real to those
Who got wounded there
Got maimed there
Died there
It was real to those who fought at Vietnam

Antietam to Vietnam
Where and when
Will it all end

Stan Platke

SHOOT OUT AT PLANET EARTH

Days of the big bad gun
Where they would meet at dawn's sun
And the slower one
Would be done

Bullets did their talking then
One shot could spell the end
And we speak of the time when
Boys were boys and men were men

It's still the same way of course
But there's a price to pay of course
Because how the West was won
Is how the world was lost

Stan Platke

POSTFACE

I went to Viet Nam a man and I came back
a boy. I am very thankful for that. As
a man I played many roles. In Viet Nam
I saw the ultimate result of role playing.
As a boy I loved a lot, very simply and
without fear. This is the first and last
thing about war that I will do. From
now on I'm going to write about things like
love as seen through the eyes of a boy.

Stan Platke

GRASS

Curious thing, grass breeds oxygen
which our cities badly need.
Grass breeds silence, which we
desperately need. Grass
may even breed ass, for all I know.
Some beautiful ass seems to crop
up in this town. But it never
seems to occur to anyone pushing
the mowers or riding them, ludicrous
little tractors, to treasure
this rough, wonder-making grass.
Whitman and Sandburg wrote poems
about it. Educational T.V.
claims it has feelings. A Virginia
professor says that heat and stink
from mowers will warm the planet,

build up carbon dioxide, do us in
just like the dinosaurs who
sixty-five million years ago
destroyed themselves with farts.
But those bastards are still
out there mowing in the rain,
mowing the grass that's already
been mowed. It was mowed yesterday.

A truck arrives, men jump down
with a whole squad of mowers.
They're on patrol. It's like Vietnam.
These bloody bastards actually think
they're keeping the economy going.
This is the only way. Blue clouds
of gas, incredible noise. Cuts off
toes, makes lovers turn from joy
to slam the window. House sides
shake, and nervous types go nuts.

My son calls from overseas to say
he's been mowing for seven hours today.
I pity him, I tell him, I never meant
for him to go that way. He says
Search and Destroy is his mission
now he is a man. There's grass
out there. I tell him I recall
what his first words were—"Help Me"—
as he was waddling toward a door
trying to open it, get out
into the air and sweet smell of grass.

David Ray

AFTER THE BOMB

There was a sadness in the land
And silence.
The northern birds had ceased to sing
And blue fire had grown in the east.

From the depths of hell blood welled
And spewed across the valleys and the plains.
Vipers came when the blood had dried
And slithered through the dead, gray grass.

Hearts were sick with longing for the color green,
But it was gone, covered in rust red and gray.
They cried out in their grief. . .
Lord, have mercy on us! We have seen the pit!

LORD, WE DID NOT UNDERSTAND.
LORD, IF WE HAD ONLY KNOWN.
Lord, let the birds sing. We will listen.
Lord, let the grass grow. We will see.

Joseph M. Shea

Paul Tick

CONTENTS

*Illustrations otherwise not attributed are
courtesy of the War Resisters League*

BIOGRAPHICAL NOTES

SAM ABRAMS teaches at Rochester Institute of Technology in Rochester, N.Y. A poet active in the Angry Arts Against the War in Vietnam. "Footnotes to Plato #2471" was in manuscript.

BRUCE ANELLO (1947-1968) was killed in Dragon Valley, Vietnam, on May 31, 1968. Poet, musician, draftee, infantry sergeant, posthumously awarded the Silver Star. His war diary first appeared in *WIN* Magazine.

JOAN BAEZ, founder of the Institute for the Study of Nonviolence in California, epitomized the key involvement of folk singers and other musicians in the Vietnam War protests. "Only You and Only Me" is from an address at an antiwar rally in Madison Square Garden in 1965.

JOHN BALABAN teaches at Penn State. Conscientious objector, two years' civilian service in Vietnam, where he learned Vietnamese and collected oral folk poetry published in *Ca Dao Vietnam* (Unicorn Press). "Mau Than" appeared in his poetry collection *After Our War* (U. of Pittsburgh Press).

JOHNNY BARANSKI is active in a Catholic Worker Community in Portland, Ore. Jailed nine months for pouring blood on Selective Service files during the Indochina War, in 1980 served six month sentence for a Trident submarine protest. "Search & Destroy" and "For Peace" are from his poetry collections *The Dawn of War* (Dorrance & Co.) and *Poems from Prison* (Sunburst Press).

JAN BARRY, a poet and journalist based in New Jersey, was a founder of Vietnam Veterans Against the War (VVAW).

ELIZABETH BARTLETT lives and writes in San Diego, Cal. "A Vote for Peace" appeared in her poetry collection, *Address in Time* (Dufour Editions).

JOHN BEECHER (1904-1980) was a poet, teacher, social activist and independent publishing pioneer. "Engagement at the Salt Fork" appeared in his *Report to the Stockholders* (Ramparts Press) and *Collected Poems, 1924-1974* (Macmillian).

JOHN BEITZEL was active in VVAW after service as an infantry sergeant in Vietnam. "Coming Home" was from a Winter Soldier Investigation hearing in Philadelphia, Pa., in 1971.

RACHELLE BENVENISTE lives and writes in Culver City, Cal. "I work in a library" was excerpted from a letter to the editor; "The Soldier" was in manuscript.

PETER BERENBAK is a newspaper advertising sales manager in Morristown, N.J. Served in army in Vietnam. "With Peace Comes Reality" appeared in the Morristown *Daily Record*. "The Garden Gate," "The Game" and "Was This All There Was To See?" were in manuscript.

BROTHER BERNARD lives and writes in Saint Leo Abbey, Fla. "New Vision" appeared in his poetry collection, *War Is Stop It* (Pasco Shopper Press).

DANIEL BERRIGAN, poet and Catholic priest, has spent much time in prison, court rooms and underground for his war resistance work. "Neither You Nor I" is from a letter to friends; other selections were excerpted from *The Dark Night of Resistance* (Doubleday) and his play *The Trial of the Catonsville Nine* (Bantam).

WENDELL BERRY is a Kentucky farmer, teacher and poet. "Dark With Power" appeared in his poetry collection *Openings* (Harcourt Brace Jovanovich).

MARGARET KEY BIGGS lives and writes in Port Saint Joseph, Fla. "Dark Growth" appeared in her poetry collection *Swampfire* (Samisdat Press); "The Demarkation Line" was in manuscript.

KARL BISSINGER is a photographer on the War Resisters League national office staff. He was arrested after photographing the disarmament banner on the White House Lawn in the "Washington 11" case.

ARTHUR S. BLANK teaches at Yale University School of Medicine. Army psychiatrist in Vietnam, active in VVAW. "Atrocity" and "Remembering Vietnam" were excerpted from an address to Veterans Administration organizers of Operation Outreach for Vietnam Veterans.

RICHARD BOYLE was a war correspondent in Indochina. "Flower of the Dragon" is excerpted from his book *Flower of the Dragon: The Breakdown of the U.S. Army in Vietnam* (Ramparts Press).

MILLEN BRAND (1906-1980) was a poet, novelist and book editor. "August 6, 1945" appeared in his poetry collection *Local Lives* (Potter); a selection of six poems appeared in his collection *Peace March* (Countryman Press); "At the Main Gate, General Dynamics, Groton" was in manuscript.

JOSEPH BRUCHAC is a poet and small press editor in Greenfield Center, N.Y. "June through September, 1963" appeared in *The Trojan Horse*; "Burn Unit" appeared in *Shenandoah*.

SALLY BUCKNER lives and writes in Raleigh, N.C. "Two Children" was in manuscript.

HAYDEN CARRUTH is a poet teaching at Syracuse University. "On Being Asked to Write a Poem Against the War in Vietnam" appeared in *Kayak 30*; "The Birds of Vietnam" appeared in his poetry collection *From Snow and Rock, From Chaos* (New Directions).

CLIFF CATTON (Newton Highlands, Mass.) was active in the American Committee to Keep Biafra Alive. "Out to Pasture" and "Counter-Recruitment" were self-published on mimeographed leaflets.

JANET CARNCROSS CHANDLER lives and writes in Auburn, Cal. "Cacaphony in State Park Campground" was in manuscript.

PAUL EUGENE CLARK (Reading, Pa.) is a poet and organizer for Mobilization for Survival. "SALT II" and "October 15, 1978" were in manuscript.

MERRITT CLIFTON is a poet and editor of *Samisdat*, published in Quebec and Vermont. "Heritage" and "R.I.P." appeared in that magazine; "Berkeley in Vietnam" was excerpted from his novella *Betrayal* (Samisdat Press).

HORACE COLEMAN is a poet teaching at Ohio University. Military service in Vietnam. "I Drive the Valiant," "Feed Me" and "Me" were in manuscript.

GEOFFREY COOK (San Francisco, Cal.) is a poet active on behalf of imprisoned Latin American writers. "Threnody for a Revolutionary" appeared in *United States: An Anthology of Political Poetry* (Buffalo Books).

KATE CORWIN lives and writes in Toledo, Ohio. "The Natives Cry" was in manuscript.

WILLIAM CRANDELL (Columbus, Ohio) was a VVAW organizer after army service in Vietnam. "Winter Soldier Investigation" was excerpted from his introduction to war crimes hearings conducted by Vietnam veterans in Detroit, Mich., published in the *Congressional Record* and *The Winter Soldier Investigation: An Inquiry into American War Crimes* (Beacon Press).

FRANK A. CROSS JR. is a California farmer and poet. Infantry sergeant in Vietnam. "Gliding Baskets" appeared in *Free Fire Zone: Short Stories by Vietnam Veterans* (1st Casualty Press); "B-52s at Home" was in manuscript.

KIM CRUMB is in second grade in Montclair, N.J. "Magic Flowers" was written at age 6.

ART CUELHO is a poet and small press editor in Big Timber, Mont. "My Country" appeared in *Goliards*; "Political Promise" was in manuscript.

DIANA DAVIES is a photographer in Roxbury, Mass. Many of her photographs appeared in *The Vietnam Songbook* (Guardian) and other chronicles of the Indochina peace movement.

REGINA DECORMIER-SHEKERJIAN is an artist and poet in New Paltz, N.Y. "1966" was in manuscript.

EMILIO DE GRAZIA lives and writes in Winona, Minn. "I Went So I Could Say I Knew" was excerpted from his short story "Little Sister Death," which was in manuscript.

DO NGHE, a pen name, was a doctor in the South Vietnamese army. "Sleep well, sleep well, my son" was excerpted from his poem "The Mother's Chant," which appeared in *Of Quiet Courage: Poems from Viet Nam* (Indochina Mobile Education Project).

ARTHUR DOBRIN lives and writes in Westbury, Long Island. "Ft. Dix, 1961" appeared in *Arts Review*.

SHARON DOUBIAGO is a California poet. "The Age of the Soldier" was excerpted from a letter to the editor; "The War Between the Sexes" and "from I Don't Want to Talk About It" were in manuscript.

FRANZ DOUSKEY is a Connecticut poet. "Cambodian Temple Rubbing" was in manuscript.

DON DUNCAN was an editor of *Ramparts* Magazine and antiwar organizer after serving in army special forces in Vietnam. "We Did a Terrible Thing" was excerpted from the Winter Soldier Investigation hearings in Detroit, Mich.

RAY DUREM (1915-1963) was a poet and social activist. U.S. Navy and Spanish Civil War veteran. "I know I'm Not Sufficiently Obscure" appeared in *The Poetry of Black America* (Harper & Row).

DON DZIENIS' "A Message in Court No. 4" appeared in the Morristown (N.J.) *Daily Record*.

W.D. EHRHART is a poet and journalist from Perkasie, Pa. Marine sergeant in Vietnam, antiwar activist. "Letter," "Dancing" and "A Confirmation" appeared in his poetry collection *The Awkward Silence* (Northwoods Press); "The Teacher" and "The Last Day" appeared in *The Samisdat Poems of W.D. Ehrhart* (Samisdat Press); "An Address to Middle America" appeared in *Fourth Dimension*.

MARGARET FLANAGAN EICHER lives and writes in Saratoga Springs, N.Y. "Personal End of a War" was in manuscript.

ROBERT BAKER ELDER is a poet, novelist and journalist in Auburn, Cal. Army veteran of WWII. "The Wake of the Second World War" was excerpted from his novel *Whom the Gods Destroy* (Comet Press).

DANIEL ELLSBERG is a writer, teacher and antiwar activist in California. Former Defense and State Department official, released the secret study of the Vietnam War known as the Pentagon Papers. "The Language of Torturers" was excerpted from his book *Papers on the War* (Simon & Schuster).

GLORIA EMERSON, a war correspondent in Vietnam, is the author of *Winners & Losers: Battles, Retreats, Gains, Losses and Ruins from a Long War* (Random House). "Amnesty?" appeared in *American Report*.

DAVID ENGDAHL is a Denver, Colo., attorney and poet active on the legal team which represents Kent State shooting victims in court actions against state officials. "Remembering Kent" was in manuscript.

MARY ENGEL lives and writes in North Bergen, N.J. "Wear Shoes" appeared in the *Berkeley Barb*.

LIZ FARRELL is a Connecticut poet. "For Timothy Clover" was in manuscript.

BOB FELDMAN (Urbana, Ill.) is a poet and composer-performer with the United Mime Workers. Conscientious objector during the Vietnam War. "Onus 2" and "Con/s/piracy" were in manuscript.

FRANK FINALE lives and writes in Pine Beach, N.J. "Exorcism" appeared in *Wind Literary Journal*.

LEAH FRITZ, a New York writer, is the author of *Thinking Like a Woman* (WIN Books). "Women Strike for Peace" was excerpted from an essay in that collection, which first appeared in the *Village Voice*.

ANDREW GLENN is a poet in Seattle, Wash. Served in army in Korea. "Korea 1968" and "Upon Hearing Uncle's War Stories" were in manuscript.

LESTER GOLDBERG lives and writes in Cranford, N.J. WWII veteran, antiwar activist. "Casualty List" was excerpted from his short story "The Early Train," which appeared in *Conn. Fireside*; "Washington Protest" was excerpted from his short story "The Beast in the Walls," which appeared in *Confrontation*.

RAFAEL JESUS GONZALEZ is a California poet. Korean War veteran, antiwar activist. "Exhortation" appeared in *Peace & Pieces: An Anthology of Contemporary American Poetry* (Peace & Pieces Foundation).

HAI HA's "Invitations" appeared in *Of Quiet Courage: Poems from Viet Nam*.

LEO HAMALIAN teaches at City College of New York. "Nursery Rhyme" appeared in *Ararat Quarterly* and *Out of the War Shadow: An Anthology of Current Poetry* (War Resisters League 1968 Peace Calendar).

EVAN HANEY was active in VVAW after navy service in Vietnam. "The American War" was excerpted from the Winter Soldier hearings in Detroit.

STEVEN HASSNA is a Vietnam War veteran and antiwar activist in California. "Saturday Rip-Off Blues," "Jungle Shirt Boogie," "Have You Felt?" and "Memories of Tomorrow" appeared in his poetry collection *Morning Coffee Shop Madness* (Rising Tree Productions).

TOM HAWKINS (Raleigh, N.C.) is a Vietnam veteran, antiwar activist. "Pax" and "Body Count Box Score" were in manuscript; "War Disease" was excerpted from a letter to the editor.

SAMUEL HAZO, in Pittsburgh, Pa. is a poet and novelist. "Battle News" appeared in *Out of the War Shadow* (War Resisters League) and his collection, *Once for the Last Bandit* (U. of Pittsburgh Press).

L. RUSSELL HERMAN JR. lives and writes in Raleigh, N.C. "The Fifteenth Day of the Fourth Month of the Year 1972" was in manuscript.

FRANK HIGGINS is a poet and photographer in Kansas City, Mo. Vietnam War veteran. "Andersonville Souvenir Thumb Screws" was in manuscript.

HOANG SON was a Saigon high school student when she wrote "They are called My," published under the title "Americans Are Not Beautiful" in *Of Quiet Courage: Poems from Viet Nam*.

PRESTON H. HOOD III is a Maine poet. Served in navy in Vietnam. "Ready to Fight, Ready to Die" was in manuscript.

SHEL HOROWITZ (Philadelphia, Pa.) is active in Mobilization for Survival. "I saw the death machines," "Death Dealers," "August 6, 1978" and "Dead Wrong" were in manuscript.

DOUG HOSTETTER, executive secretary of the New England Region of the American Service Committee, served three years with Vietnam Christian Service. Some of his photographs included here appeared in *WIN* Magazine, *New World Outlook* and *Hostages of War* (Indochina Mobile Education Project).

AL HUBBARD was active in VVAW after air force service in Vietnam. "America" appeared in *The Winter Soldier Investigation* (Beacon Press).

RICHARD HUGHES, a New York actor, organized and directed hostels for orphaned street children in Vietnam for eight years. "The Vietnam Legacy" was in manuscript.

SADIE WERNICK HURWITZ lives and writes in Los Angeles, Cal. "June Twenty Third in the City of the Angels in the Year of Our Lord One Thousand Nine Hundred and Sixty Seven" was in manuscript.

RUTH HARRIET JACOBS is a poet and professor of sociology at Boston University. "Twenty Years After" appeared in the Church of the Larger Fellowship *Bulletin*.

SUSU JEFFREY (San Francisco, Cal.) is a poet active with Mobilization for Survival. "Substitute History" and "War Baby Remembers Hitler" were in manuscript.

DONAS JOHN lives and writes in Palms, Cal. "Winter Soldiers" appeared in *North Country Anvil*.

DEBORAH KEENAN lives and writes in St. Paul, Minn. "How I Will Know When the War Is Over" was in manuscript.

WILLIAM G. KELSEY won discharge as a conscientious objector after graduation from the U.S. Naval Academy during the Vietnam War. "To Learn from Hiroshima" appeared in *The Progressive*; "Application for Discharge as a Consciencious Objector" was in manuscript.

JOHN KERRY, a Massachusetts attorney, was active in VVAW after navy service in Vietnam. "Testimony to Congress" was excerpted from Senate Foreign Relations Committee proceedings which appeared in the *Congressional Record*.

WALKER KNIGHT (Atlanta, Ga.) is a director of the Home Mission Board of the Southern Baptist Convention. "The Peacemaker" appeared in *Home Missions*. The poem was quoted in part by President Carter during the signing of the Israeli-Egyptian Peace Treaty at the White House in 1979.

GEORGE KNOWLTON is a Rhode Island artist and antiwar activist. Served in army in Germany.

HARRISON KOHLER is a poet and attorney in Atlanta, Ga. Vietnam veteran antiwar activist. "Combating the Love of War" was excerpted from his book of essays *It Is Well: Reflections on War* (Brandon Press).

RON KOVIC (Los Angeles, Cal.) was active in VVAW after service in Vietnam as a marine sergeant. "Kent State" was excerpted from his book *Born on the Fourth of July* (McGraw-Hill).

STEVE KOWIT lives and writes in San Diego, Cal. Draft dodger during Vietnam War. "They will not forget us" appeared in *10,000 Corpses* (Proexistence Press).

JAMES D. LANGE (Madison, Wis.) is a poet and psychiatric social worker. Army medic in Vietnam. "Violence," "Vietnamese belong in school," "Nightmares" and "Hope" were in manuscript.

S. LEE is a poet and small press editor in Dublin, Ca. "Letter from Nam" appeared in *California Quarterly*.

CORNEL LENGYEL lives and writes in El Dorado National Forest, Cal. Poet, teacher, small press editor. "Petition" appeared in his play *The Atom Clock*.

DENISE LEVERTOV is a poet and teacher in Massachusetts. Editor of the War Resisters League's 1968 Peace Calendar — *Out of the War Shadow: An Anthology of Current Poetry*. "The Day the Audience Walked Out on Me, and Why," "In Thai Binh (Peace) Province" and "To Stay Alive" are from her poetry collections *Footprints, The Freeing of the Dust* and *To Stay Alive* (New Directions).

RICHARD LEVINE is a poet and journalist in Greenwich, N.Y. Vietnam veteran. "Veteran's Day" and "Spoils of War" were in manuscript.

CHUCK LOGAN is an artist in St. Paul, Minn. Active in VVAW after army service in Vietnam.

WALTER LOWENFELS (1897-1976) was a poet, journalist and editor of several social protest poetry anthologies, including *Where is Vietnam?* (Anchor Books) and *The Writing on the Wall* (Doubleday). "American Voices" is from his poetry collection *American Voices* (Roving Eye Press).

DON LUCE served over a dozen years in Vietnam with International Voluntary Services, other civilian aid agencies and as a journalist. Coeditor of two Vietnamese poetry anthologies, *We Promise One Another* and *Of Quiet Courage*, published by Indochina Mobile Education Project, which he helped organize. "Christmas Eve" and "America: December 1972" appeared in his poetry collection *Shadows from a Cabin Night* (Asian Center).

ALAN LUPACK is a poet in Wayne, Neb. Vietnam veteran. "Army Experience" and "The Ballad of Basic Training" were in manuscript.

PETER MAHONEY is a poet in Brooklyn, N.Y. Active in VVAW after army service in Vietnam. "Calley and that Old Bitterness" appeared in the *New York Times*; "To My Younger Brother" was in manuscript.

MIRIAM C. MALOY lives and writes in Aptos, Cal. "A Different Drum" was in manuscript.

MILTON C. MAPES (Washington, D.C.) is executive director of the National Peace Academy Campaign. U.S. Naval Academy graduate, WWII veteran. "For a U.S. Peace Academy" was excerpted from an essay titled "To Move the Whole Future" in *Anthropology and Humanism Quarterly*.

HERBERT WOODWARD MARTIN is a poet teaching at the University of Dayton. "A Negro Soldier's Viet Nam Diary" appeared in *The Poetry of Black America* (Harper & Row).

DOUGLAS MICHAEL MASSING is a California poet. "Some Tomorrows" was in manuscript.

MILTON MAYER is roving editor of *The Progressive*. "What the Army Builds" and "Postscript" were excerpted from essays in that magazine.

GERALD MCCARTHY is a poet in Chili, N.Y. Vietnam veteran antiwar activist. "Marking Time" was in manuscript.

JESUS PAPOLETO MELENDEZ is a poet in the Bronx, N.Y. "And Doves Were Nowhere to be Found" appeared in *Greenfield Review*; "Story from a Mountain" was in manuscript.

JEFFREY MILLER (1950-1970) was one of the students killed by national guardsmen at Kent State University.

JANET N. NEUMAN (Washington, D.C.) is 86 and still an active war protester and poet. "My Mind Says No!" appeared in her poetry collection *Today, Tomorrow & Yesterday*.

NGO VINH LONG is a poet and historian in Massachusetts. "on this land" appeared on an antiwar poster during the Vietnam War.

THICH NHAT HANH is a poet and Buddhist monk in exile in France. Led the Vietnamese Buddhist Peace Delegation in Paris. "Listen to this" was excerpted from his poem "Condemnation" which appeared in his collection, *Viet Nam Poems* (Unicorn Press); "Resolution" and "Recommendation" appeared in his collection *The Cry of Vietnam* (Unicorn Press).

JOAN NICHOLSON lives and writes in Ithaca, N.Y. Served time in prison for anti-draft board action. "We're Leaving Indochina" was in manuscript.

DON OGDEN is a poet in Wellfleet, Mass. Active in anti-nuclear movement. "Enola Gay" appeared in his poetry collection, *Fuel Cycle Blues*.

GRACE PALEY is a short story writer, poet and teacher active in the War Resisters League. Her statement to the court in the "Washington 11" case appeared in *WRL News.*

JIM PATHE is a photographer in Madison, N.J. Navy veteran, active in Veterans For Peace in Vietnam.

JOHN PILGER is a British journalist based in London. "The Gook-Hunter" appeared in the *New York Times.*

STAN PLATKE is a St. Louis, Mo., attorney and poet. Active in VVAW after army service in Vietnam. "Antietam to Vietnam," "Shoot Out at Planet Earth" and "Postface" appeared in his poetry collection *Antietam to Vietnam* (Theater in Translation).

WILLIAM POWERS lives and writes in Buffalo, N.Y. Marine Corps veteran. "Truth" was excerpted from his short story "Ascent to Truth," which was in manuscript.

SANDY PRIMM is a writer and social activist in Rolla, Mo. VVAW organizer after army service in Vietnam. "Tim," "The Peace of God," "Radicalization" and "For a Russian" appeared in his book *Short Time* (Cauldron Press).

SHELDON RAMSDELL is a photographer and journalist from Ogunquit, Maine. Active in VVAW after navy service in Southeast Asia.

DAVID RAY is a poet teaching at the University of Missouri in Kansas City. Coeditor of *A Poetry Reading Against the Vietnam War* (Sixties Press). "Inductees on the Plane" appeared in *Chicago Review;* "Grass" was in manuscript.

DAVID ALLEN REED was sentenced to three years in prison for draft resistance in the Indochina War. Active in SDS at Harvard, Committee for Nonviolent Action and other peace campaigns.

JULIE ROBBINS is a poet and art student in Cambridge, Mass. "Captions" was in manuscript.

LARRY ROTTMANN is a poet and novelist in Cambridge, Idaho. VVAW organizer after army service in Vietnam. "Hey! Remember me?" appeared in the *Congressional Record* report on the Winter Soldier hearings in Detroit.

MURIEL RUKEYSER (1913-1980) was a poet, teacher and social activist. "Peace the great meaning," "Hostages" and "Bringing" appeared in her *Collected Poems* (McGraw-Hill).

REG SANER is a poet teaching at the University of Colorado in Boulder. Korean War veteran. "Ancient Fragment from the Edge of the Empire" appeared in *The Minnesota Review.*

TEO SAVORY is a poet, novelist and editor of Unicorn Press in Greensboro, N.C. "The Children Come" appeared in *The Catholic Worker*; her translation of "Strangers Estranged" by Jacques Prevert appeared in *Words for All Seasons* (Unicorn Press).

JOHN SCHAFER served four years in Vietnam with International Voluntary Services. "Hoa Binh" appeared in the IVS Newsletter.

TOM SCHMIDT is a poet and musician in Fair Oaks, Cal. "Cadaver 1467" appeared in *Mutiny Does Not Happen Lightly: The Literature of the American Resistance to the Vietnam War* (Scarecrow Press) and under the title "Butter" in *New American & Canadian Poetry* (Beacon Press).

E.M. SCHORB is a poet in Brooklyn, N.Y. "Dirge for the Dead Students" appeared in nis collection *The Poor Boy and Other Poems* (Dragon's Teeth Press).

BOB SEELEY is editor of CCCO (Central Committee for Conscientious Objectors) *News Notes*. "Another Napoleon's March on Moscow?" was excerpted from a letter to potential CCCO supporters.

JOSEPH M. SHEA is a poet in Washington, D.C. Vietnam veteran. "Comfortable people don't look" and "After the Bomb" were in manuscript.

GILBERT SORRENTINO is a poet and novelist. "Retreat" appeared in *Out of the War Shadow*.

LAUREL SPEER is a poet and short story writer in Tucson, Arizona. "An Event in Asia" was in manuscript.

FRANK STEWART is a poet in Honolulu, Hawaii. Draft exile in Sweden during Vietnam War. "Black Winter" was in manuscript.

KATHLEEN STILWELL is a poet and artist in Ames, Iowa.

ANNIE STINE is a poet, printer and graphic artist in San Francisco, Cal. "Standing Like the End of War" was in manuscript.

PETER STOOL (1947-1975) was active in VVAW after military service in Indochina. "Our Sole Nourishment Is Hope" was excerpted from his hospital diary, which appeared in *Fellowship*.

A. SWANSON is a poet in Enfield, Conn. Vietnam veteran. "Song of the Century" was in manuscript.

HILLMAN TAYLOR lives and writes in Dallas, Texas. "Voices at a Convention" was in manuscript.

PAUL TICK is a photographer in Jamaica, N.Y. A founder of Artists for Survival. His photographs, "Stop War" and "What Do You Do In Case of a Nuclear Accident" appear on postcards distributed by movement organizations.

TRAN VAN DINH teaches at Temple University. Former soldier, cabinet officer and diplomat for various Vietnamese governments. "Tet in the Year of the Tiger" appeared in *The Christian Century*; "From Eagle to Spring" appeared in the *New York Times*.

TRINH CONG SON's "A thousand years of Chinese reign" is from his folk song "The Heritage of Our Motherland," which appeared in *We Promise One Another: Poems from an Asian War* (Indochina Mobile Education Project).

LINDA KAY VANDERBERG is a poet in Houston, Texas. "Although I was not a soldier and therefore not a veteran, I am a victim," she writes, "having lost two loved ones." "Amnesty" was in manuscript.

R.B. WEBER is a poet teaching at Southampton College of Long Island University. Korean War veteran. "On a bridge at Hiroshima" was in manuscript.

ED WHITE is a poet in Security, Colo. "Veteran" was in manuscript.

DOUG YAMAMOTO is a poet in San Francisco, Cal. "My Lai," "If Asians Have Been Quiet" and "At the Red River" were in manuscript.

RUBIN ZAR lives and writes in Chula Vista, Cal. "Tombstones" and "The 69th Regiment" were in manuscript.

Illustration by **Rocky Flats Nuclear Weapons Facility Project.**

NOTE TO THE READER

What is the purpose of poetry is like asking what is the purpose of peace. But the question, inevitably, rises over any literary work aimed at challenging government actions.

Some readers will sputter that "art and politics don't mix," as though artists somehow lived and died differently from the rest of the family. It's an old argument, and beside the point.

After thirty-seven years' rude awakening to the eggshell fragility of life let alone art in this century of world wars, mass political hysteria, assassinations, mass murder, concentration camps, blacklisting witch-hunts and genocide, increasingly overshadowed by the specter of atomic annihilation, perhaps of all life for all time, I have come to this modest conclusion:

What's the point of poetry?
Might as well ask what's the point of spring.
What's the point of a flower opening,
what's the point of singing?

Might as well ask why a bird flies,
why a tree seeks the sky.
(That's the way life lies.)

It used to be that poets (like the rest of humanity) longed for immortality, if not for themselves at least for their poetry. Now it would be enough, for any compassionate poet, just to know that the earth and its unraveling mantle of life will survive: For what possible hope (or glory) would there be in dreaming of our poems surviving lying buried in a lifeless, spinning wasteland.

Late in World War I, English poet Wilfred Owen returned to the trenches to speak out for the other suffering soldiers, to write his now famous acerbic poems against war's madness. "And am I not myself a conscientious objector with a very seared conscience?" the young infantry officer earlier had written home from a military hospital. Wilfred Owen died on the battlefield just days before the armistice was signed. With his last poems (which to later generations of readers in England and elsewhere have come to symbolize the wasteland of the First World War) he left a note, the essence of which was: "All a poet can do today is warn."

Poets and other war protesters today can do no less. And perhaps, by making it clear that in the atomic-weapons age all life is now in the trenches, hopefully there is still time for those of us living to do more. . .to help rally our fellow humans to work out a lasting armistice.

J.B.

organizations have no purpose
are only alphabets
if your purpose is death
you put together letters to form the word
pentagon
which is how you spell war

in 1923 those women (and it is
a clarity of history, not a token
gesture, which puts women in first place
here) and men
who had risked riots
prison and lynching
to oppose the first world war
formed war resisters league

the purpose of people is living
dying only when necessary
and killing
never

to resist all war
poverty is war
racism is war
rape is an act of war
as surely as wild shrapnel
prisons are war
capitalism is war

we have declared we are at peace with all people
and at war with all institutions which seek to
arm us which seek to repress us to exploit us
to kill us
beginning with the institution of war
so as an act of our war
we have put down our guns
choosing the enormous risks of love

for that purpose war resisters league was formed
you are its purpose

For further information/action:

American Friends Service Committee
1501 Cherry St.
Philadelphia, PA 19102

Asian Center/Clergy & Laity Concerned
198 Broadway, Rm. 302
New York, NY 10038

Bulletin of Concerned Asian Scholars
P.O. Box W
Charlemont, MA. 01339

CCCO (Central Committee for Conscientious Objectors)
2208 South St.
Philadelphia, PA 19146

Fellowship Magazine/Fellowship of Reconciliation
Box 271
Nyack, NY 10960

Indochina Curriculum Group
11 Garden Street
Cambridge, Ma. 02138

National Peace Academy Campaign
1625 Eye St., N.W.-Suite 726
Washington, DC 20006

The Progressive Magazine
408 W. Gorham St.
Madison, WI 53703

Samisdat Magazine
Box 129
Richford, VT 05476

SANE
514 C St., N.E.
Washington, DC 20002

Southeast Asia Resource Center
P.O. Box 4000D
Berkeley, CA. 94704

Unicorn Press
Box 3307
Greensboro, NC 27402

War Resisters League
339 Lafayette St.
New York, NY 10012

War Resisters League/West
85 Carl St.
San Francisco, CA 94117

WIN Magazine
326 Livingston St.
Brooklyn, NY 11217

Women Strike for Peace
145 S. 13 St.
Philadelphia, PA 19107

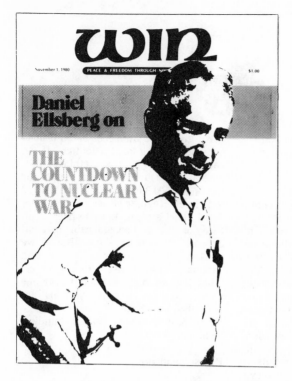

Box 129
Richford, Vermont
05476   U.S.A.

SAMISDAT

Box 10
Brigham, Quebec
J0E 1J0   Canada

SAMISDAT is not just a collection of objectively 'good' writing, distinguished by style alone, with no purpose beyond display. Rather, SAMISDAT writing distinguishes itself through passion, purpose, and commitment. We live to encourage life, and to oppose whatever destroys life, on whatever pretext. We respect the laws of nature, not of government; the morals of practical consideration, 'do unto others as ye would have others do unto you,' not those of superstitious dictate. We salute no flag, obey no draft, neither take nor contribute to public funds, kneel only to tend our garden, & thumb our noses at all propriety. We see monopoly capitalism and state socialism both as slavery, founded upon violence and disrespect of human worth. We say to hell with Big Brother and his threat of nuclear apocalypse. We anticipate a solar world running through voluntary association and enlightened free enterprise, with profits measured by life quality, not just the Almighty Buck. This, indeed, is how we do business. We seek your subscriptions, and need them, surviving on a cash income averaging 37 cents an hour for fulltime work. But even more, we seek your philosophical sympathy. We have discovered and helped establish many significant writers, yet this is not the place for those after fame and fortune first. Nor do our contributors write to kill time, from boredom or as strictly personal purgative. Our authors instead share a dream; SAMISDAT gives it form; the future gives it substance.

We give all manuscript submissions our prompt, personal attention. If we can help, we do so. If something's shit, we say so. Our preferred length for fiction is 1,500-3,000 words; for poetry, 2 to 50 lines. Regular issues contain from 3 to 7 short stories, 15 to 40 poems, an essay or two, and considerable original artwork. Between regular issues we publish single-author books and chapbooks addressing similar themes. Since 1973 we have averaged over one publication per month. No. 100 appeared in mid-1980.

We mail to subscribers in bundles, semi-quarterly.

Please send me:

_____ Sample copy ($2.00)
_____ Sample copy plus our philosophy
        of writing ($2.50)
_____ Next 500 pages ($12.00)
_____ Next 1,000 pages ($20.00)
_____ All future items ($100.00)
(An average year's production is about 750 pages.)
My check or money-order accompanies. My address is:

Name:

Street or box:

City:

State or province:

Zip or postal code:

THE PHŒNIX

(From JOURNAL OF MODERN LITERATURE*)*

THE PHŒNIX is surely one of the most important magazines presently being published in America—but it's difficult to pigeon-hole. "Journal of radical pacifism" comes close, but cannot suggest the real diversity of opinion as well as the profound humanism which informs every issue. If you have the money for only a half-dozen "little magazines" this should be one of them, a bargain at

	Individuals	*Libraries*
U.S.A. & Canada	$12.00	$16.00
Overseas (surface fail)	$16.00	$20.00
Overseas (air-mail)	$20.00	$25.00

Morning Star Farm West Whately
RFD Haydenville Massachusetts 01039

UNICORN PRESS / P.O. BOX 3307 / GREENSBORO, N. C. 27402

CA DAO VIETNAM: *A Bilingual Anthology of Viet-*
namese Folk Poetry

Edited, transcribed and translated by
John Balaban

WOODBLOCK BY VO-DINH

CA DAO (pronounced "ka yow" in the
South of Vietnam, "ka zow" in the North)
are an ancient yet still current part of
Vietnamese culture, a tradition handed
down orally for many hundreds of years.
The forty-eight *ca dao* published bilin-
gually in this anthology were collected by
John Balaban while he was in Vietnam
during the war. In his ten-page introduction, Professor Balaban describes how he
taped, transcribed, and then translated
these poems. He tells about the people who
sang them and he devotes several pages
to the history and prosody of *ca dao*. The
photographs he took of some of the singers, on Phoenix Island in the Mekong
Delta, are included.

_____Cloth, illus. d.j. $15.00
_____Paper, sewn, illus. cover $ 5.00

DANIEL BERRIGAN, *Prison Poems.* 128 Pages. Intro. by
Philip Berrigan. "Berrigan's most mature poetry,"
PUBLISHERS WEEKLY
_____Cloth (sewn) only, *jacket photo* $ 7.50

TEO SAVORY, *Transitions.* Author's third poetry sequence.
Woodblock by Vo-Dinh.
_____Paper only $ 2.50

UNICORN JOURNAL (Teo Savory, editor)
prose, poetry, graphics, translations
Vol. III, paper _____$3.00   Vol. IV, paper _____$3.00

THE AWKWARD SILENCE

Poems by W.D. Ehrhart

"We are your sons, America,
and you cannot change that.
When you awake,
we will still be here."

Other Publications Available from East River Anthology

Winning Hearts & Minds: War Poems by Vietnam Veterans (1st Casualty Press/McGraw-Hill, 1972), edited by Larry Rottmann, Jan Barry and Basil T. Paquet. ''. . . one of the most anguished literary works to come out of the American experience in Southeast Asia'' (Chicago Sun-Times); ''. . . not only a collection of poetry by Vietnam War veterans, it is also a test of your humanity'' (New York Times Book Review); ''. . . the most eloquent statement of what the war is that I have seen from its participants'' (Newsweek). $1.95

Free Fire Zone: Short Stories by Vietnam Veterans (1st Casualty Press/McGraw-Hill, 1973), edited by Wayne Karlin, Basil T. Paquet and Larry Rottmann. ''Here. . . are the nightmares which all the radios in America cannot erase. . . almost more than America can bear to know about itself'' (Harper's). $2.95

Demilitarized Zones: Veterans After Vietnam (East River Anthology), edited by Jan Barry and W.D. Ehrhart. Listed as one of the ''Best Titles of 1976'' by Library Journal; ''Send for this book: it is a new species of American poetry'' (San Francisco Bay Guardian); ''It is impossible to summarize or to convey in prose the power, the terror, the anger which is the stuff of (DMZ)'' (The Nation). $2.95

Order from:

East River Anthology
75 Gates Ave., Montclair, N.J. 07042

FACULTY PRESS, INC., BROOKLYN, N.Y.